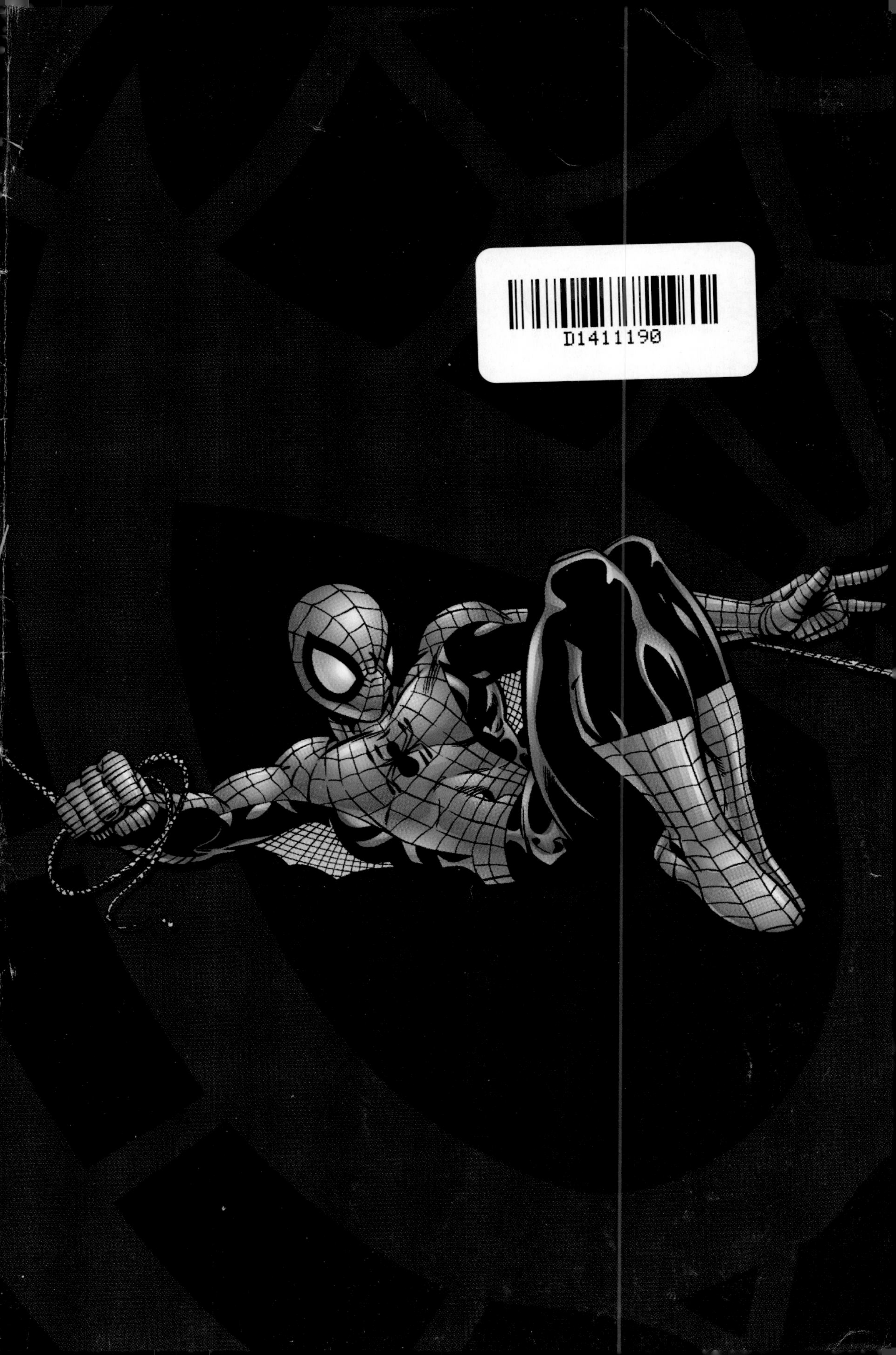

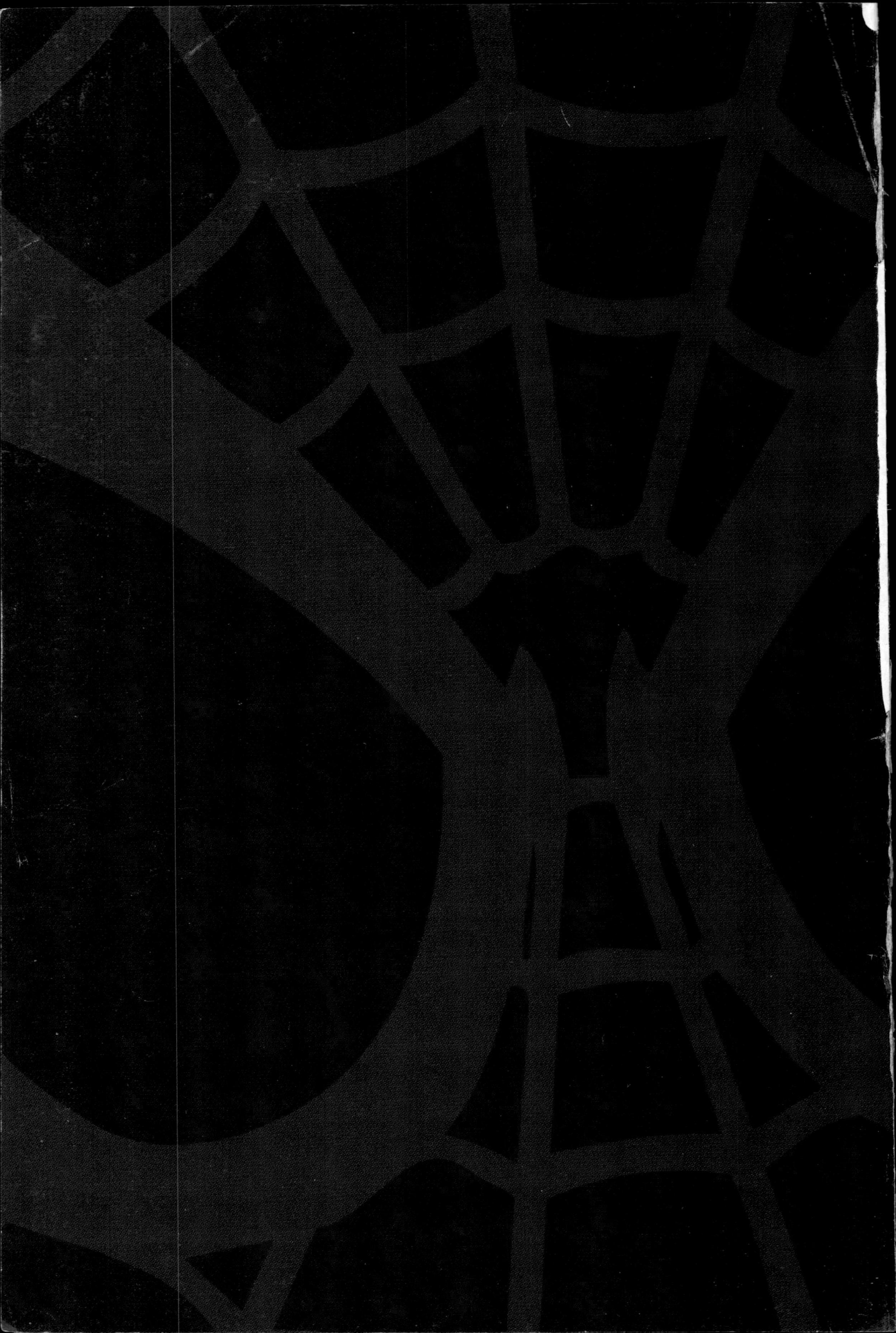

PETER PARKER: SPIDER-MAN

One Small Break

Paul Jenkins
WRITER

Mark Buckingham
PENCILS

Dan Green & Wayne Faucher
INKS

Axel Alonso
EDITOR

Kaare Andrews
COVER ART

Joe Quesada
EDITOR IN CHIEF

Bill Jemas
PRESIDENT

Bob Greenberger Director: PUBLISHING OPERATIONS

Ben Abernathy & Matty Ryan SPECIAL PROJECTS MANAGER

Stefano Perrone, Jr. MANUFACTURING REPRESENTATIVE

Patrick McGrath BOOK DESIGNER

Jessica Schwartz PRODUCTION ASSISTANT

PETER PARKER: SPIDER-MAN® ONE SMALL BREAK. Contains material originally published in magazine form as PETER PARKER: SPIDER-MAN #s 27-28 and 30-34. ISBN # 0-7851-0824-6. GST. #R127032852. Published by MARVEL COMICS, a division of MARVEL ENTERTAINMENT GROUP, INC. OFFICE OF PUBLICATION: 10 EAST 40th STREET, NEW YORK, NY 10016. Copyright © 2001 Marvel Characters, Inc. No similarity between any of the names, characters, persons, and/or institutions in this publication with those of any living or dead person or institutions is intended, and any such similarity which may exist is purely coincidental. This publication may not be sold except by authorized dealers and is sold subject to the conditions that it shall not be sold or distributed with any part of its cover or markings removed, nor in a mutilated condition. SPIDER-MAN (including all prominent characters featured in this publication and the distinctive likenesses thereof) is a trademark of MARVEL CHARACTERS, INC. Printed in Canada. PETER CUNEO, Chief Executive Officer; AVI ARAD, Chief Creative Officer; GUI KARYO, Chief Information Officer; BOB GREENBERGER, Director – Publishing Operations; STAN LEE, Chairman Emeritus.

10 9 8 7 6 5 4 3 2 1

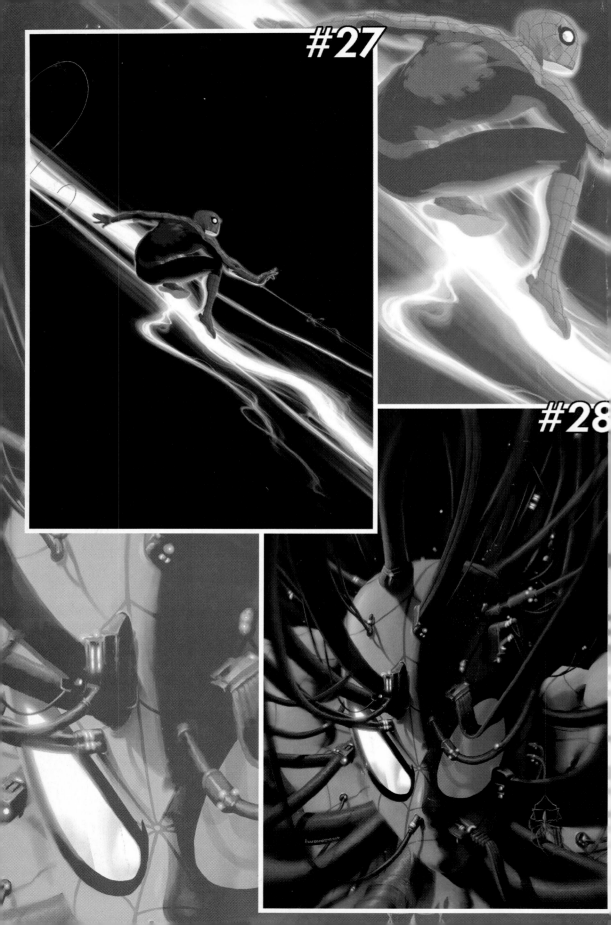

T A demonstration on Radiation, high school student PETER PARKER was bitten by an Irradiated Spider from which he gained the Arachnid's Incredible Abilities. When a burglar killed his beloved Uncle Ben, a grief-stricken Peter vowed to use his Great Powers in the service of his fellow man, because he learned an valuable lesson: With Great Power must also come Great Responsibility. S T A N L E E P R E S E N T S:

PETER PARKER SPIDER-MAN

GETTING AHEAD

I READ THIS *BOOK* ONCE -- IT WAS CALLED "HOW TO GET AHEAD."

THE KEY TO SUCCESS, SAID THE AUTHOR, IS TO GET OUT OF BED WITH A *SMILE* -- THAT'S HALF THE BATTLE WON, APPARENTLY. THE *OTHER HALF* IS TO BE AN HONEST ENOUGH PERSON THAT YOU CAN FALL ASLEEP AGAIN AT THE END OF THE DAY.

ME, I'M AN HONEST GUY.

THAT DOESN'T MEAN I SLEEP WELL AT NIGHT.

PAUL JENKINS Writer MARK BUCKINGHAM Penciler GREEN/RAMOS/BUCKINGHAM Inkers JOE ROSAS Colors
RICHARD STARKINGS & COMICRAFT'S JASON LEVINE Letters AXEL ALONSO Editor JOE QUESADA Chief

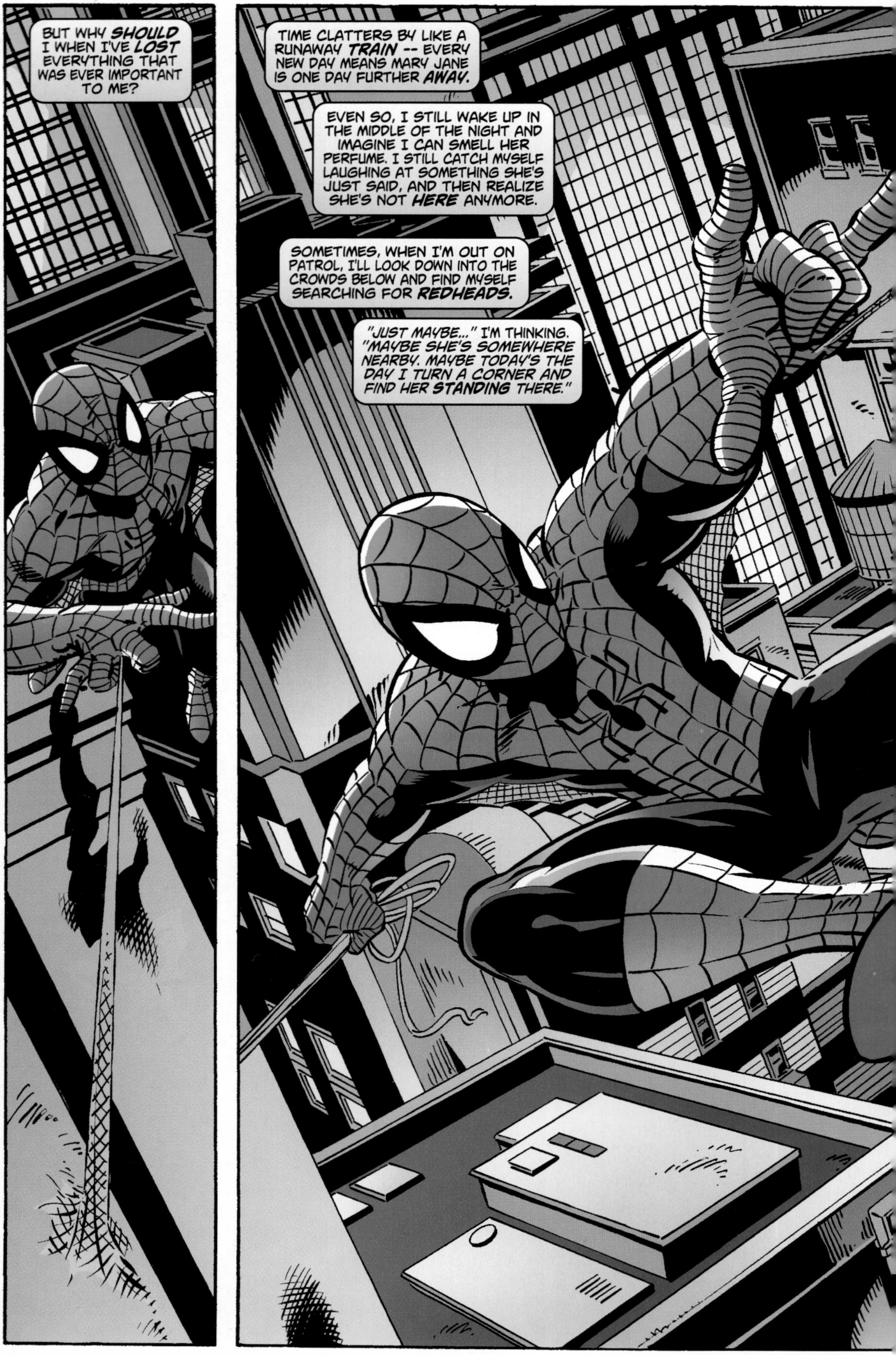

BUT WHY SHOULD I WHEN I'VE LOST EVERYTHING THAT WAS EVER IMPORTANT TO ME?
TIME CLATTERS BY LIKE A RUNAWAY TRAIN -- EVERY NEW DAY MEANS MARY JANE IS ONE DAY FURTHER AWAY.
EVEN SO, I STILL WAKE UP IN THE MIDDLE OF THE NIGHT AND IMAGINE I CAN SMELL HER PERFUME. I STILL CATCH MYSELF LAUGHING AT SOMETHING SHE'S JUST SAID, AND THEN REALIZE SHE'S NOT HERE ANYMORE.
SOMETIMES, WHEN I'M OUT ON PATROL, I'LL LOOK DOWN INTO THE CROWDS BELOW AND FIND MYSELF SEARCHING FOR REDHEADS.
"JUST MAYBE..." I'M THINKING. "MAYBE SHE'S SOMEWHERE NEARBY. MAYBE TODAY'S THE DAY I TURN A CORNER AND FIND HER STANDING THERE."

AND THEN I WONDER: WHAT IF SHE REALLY *WERE?*

SOMETHING'S HAPPENED... SOMETHING THAT'S MADE ME QUESTION *EVERYTHING.* I THINK THE GOBLIN HAS POISONED MY MIND.

I HAD HIM DOWN. I WAS GOING TO *FINISH* HIM ONCE AND FOR ALL. "YOU'LL NEVER *BEAT* ME," I SHOUTED. "YOU NEVER COULD, AND YOU NEVER WILL."

HE SIMPLY LOOKED ME IN THE EYE AS IF HE FELT *SORRY* FOR ME. "I JUST *DID,*" HE SAID.

AND THE THING IS, I THINK HE WAS *RIGHT.*

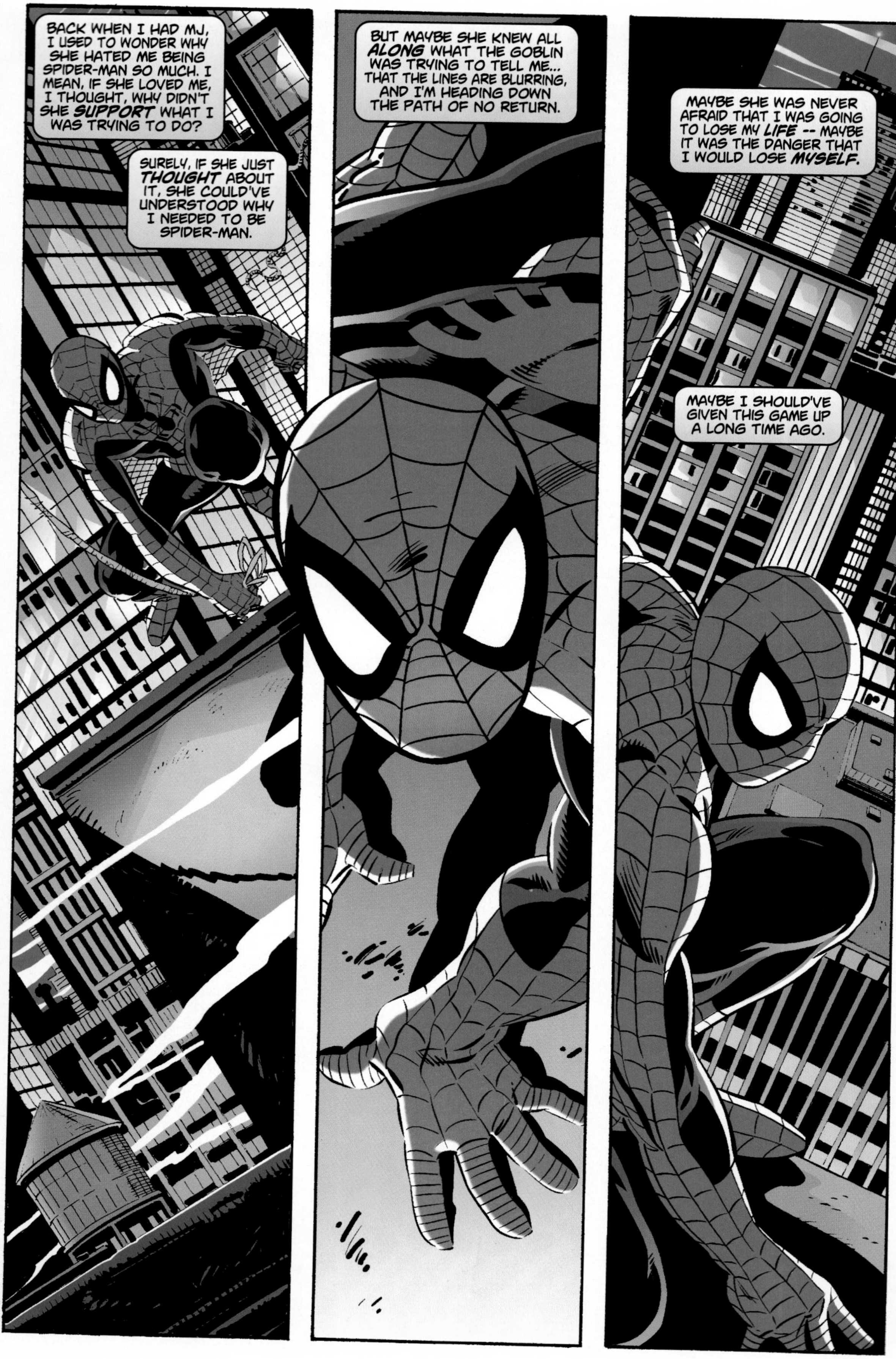
BACK WHEN I HAD MJ, I USED TO WONDER WHY SHE HATED ME BEING SPIDER-MAN SO MUCH. I MEAN, IF SHE LOVED ME, I THOUGHT, WHY DIDN'T SHE SUPPORT WHAT I WAS TRYING TO DO?
SURELY, IF SHE JUST THOUGHT ABOUT IT, SHE COULD'VE UNDERSTOOD WHY I NEEDED TO BE SPIDER-MAN.
BUT MAYBE SHE KNEW ALL ALONG WHAT THE GOBLIN WAS TRYING TO TELL ME... THAT THE LINES ARE BLURRING, AND I'M HEADING DOWN THE PATH OF NO RETURN.
MAYBE SHE WAS NEVER AFRAID THAT I WAS GOING TO LOSE MY LIFE -- MAYBE IT WAS THE DANGER THAT I WOULD LOSE MYSELF.
MAYBE I SHOULD'VE GIVEN THIS GAME UP A LONG TIME AGO.

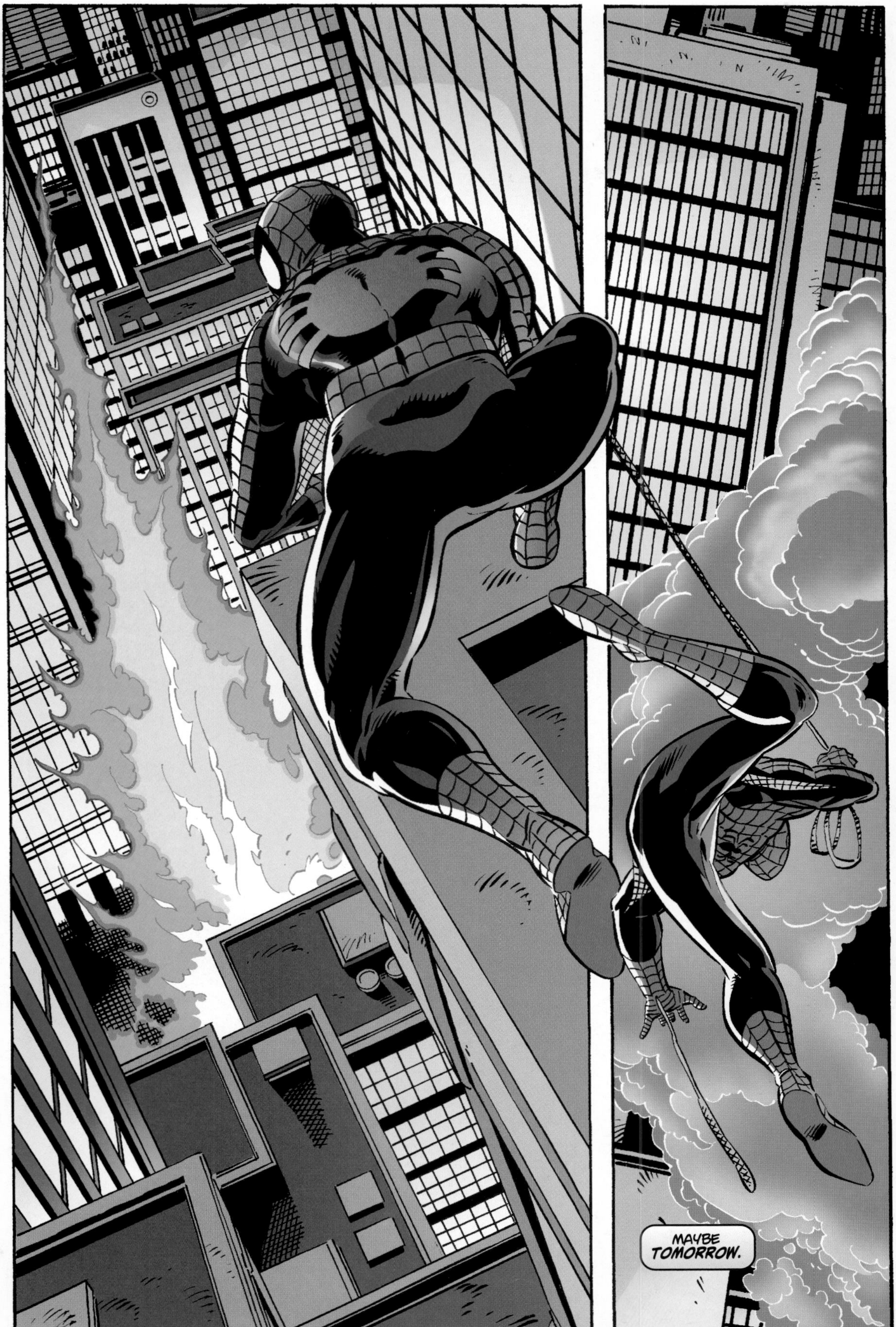
MAYBE TOMORROW.

-- OHMIGOD, DID ANYONE SEE WHAT HAPPENED? THERE WAS THIS HUGE FLASH OF *LIGHTNING* --

...IT WASN'T MY FAULT -- THE LIGHT CHANGED TO GREEN, I *SWEAR* IT DID!

NO WAY! MY LIGHT WAS GREEN --!

...A *BOMB*, OR SOMETHIN', OFFICER. NEXT THING I KNEW, THE GAS TANK *EXPLODED*...

BMMAAAP

HEY, *CHARLIE!* WE GOTTA GET THESE PEOPLE OUT AN' CORDON OFF THE AREA -- IT'S SOME KINDA ELECTRICAL *SURGE*, OR SOMETHIN', AND GET THE POWER COMPANY ON THE HORN, OKAY?

DON'T JUST STAND THERE -- *MOVE!*

YO, FELLAS! ANYTHING I CAN DO TO HELP?

FELLAS?

HMM... WHAT A ROUSING CHORUS OF INDIFFERENCE. I MUST BE LOSING MY APPEAL --

BZZZON

-YOW!

MAN... WHAT IN THE NAME OF SAM HILL IS GOING ON AROUND HERE?

THEN I SEE IT, COMING FROM ABOVE. THE SOURCE OF THE ELECTRICAL SURGES SEEMS TO BE LOCALIZED AT THE MAIN SCREEN ABOVE THE SQUARE.

KOBRA KOLA

MY SENSES ARE TINGLING... THERE HAS TO BE A WAY TO CUT OFF THE FLOW TO THE SCREEN...

...THAT POWER COUPLING!

SENSES GOING INTO *OVERDRIVE* NOW. AIR'S FULL OF PLASMA AND IONIZED GASSES... THERE'S SOMETHING *WEIRD* ABOUT THE WAY THE ELECTRICITY'S COMING DOWN AROUND US.

I ♥ NY

THIS IS NO *ORDINARY* SURGE -- IF I REMEMBER MY HIGH SCHOOL PHYSICS CORRECTLY, THE ELECTRICAL DISCHARGE SHOULD WANT TO FOLLOW THE *PATH OF LEAST RESISTANCE.*

THAT MEANS IT SHOULD BE HITTING THE METAL OBJECTS CLOSEST TO THE SOURCE OF THE SURGE.

IT SHOULD BE... BUT IT'S *NOT.* IT'S REACHING ALL THE WAY DOWN TO THE STREET.

AS IF SOMEONE -- OR *SOMETHING* -- IS *GUIDING* IT.

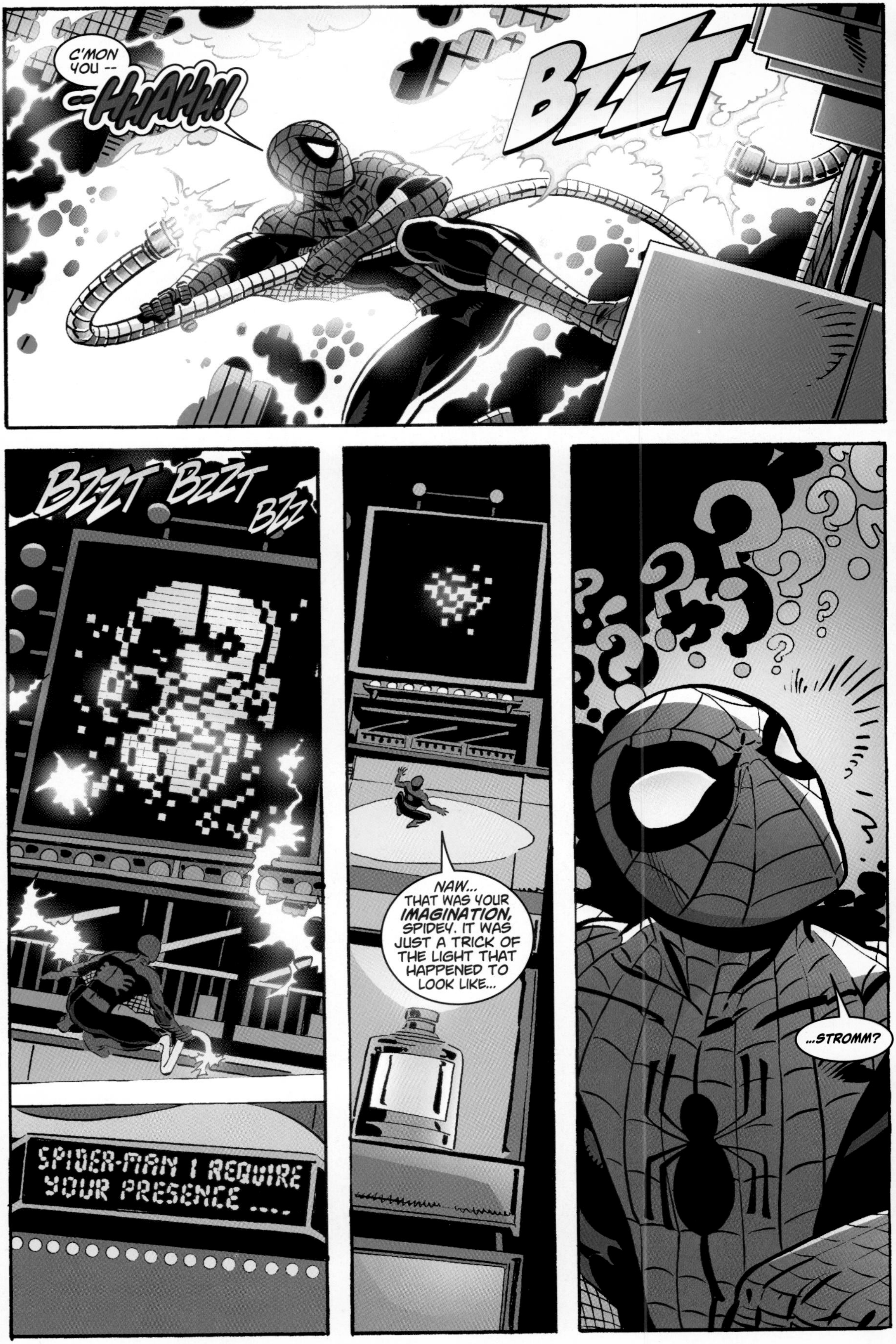
C'MON YOU --
--HHAHH!!
BZZT
BZZT BZZT BZZ
SPIDER-MAN I REQUIRE YOUR PRESENCE ....
NAW... THAT WAS YOUR IMAGINATION, SPIDEY. IT WAS JUST A TRICK OF THE LIGHT THAT HAPPENED TO LOOK LIKE...
...STROMM?

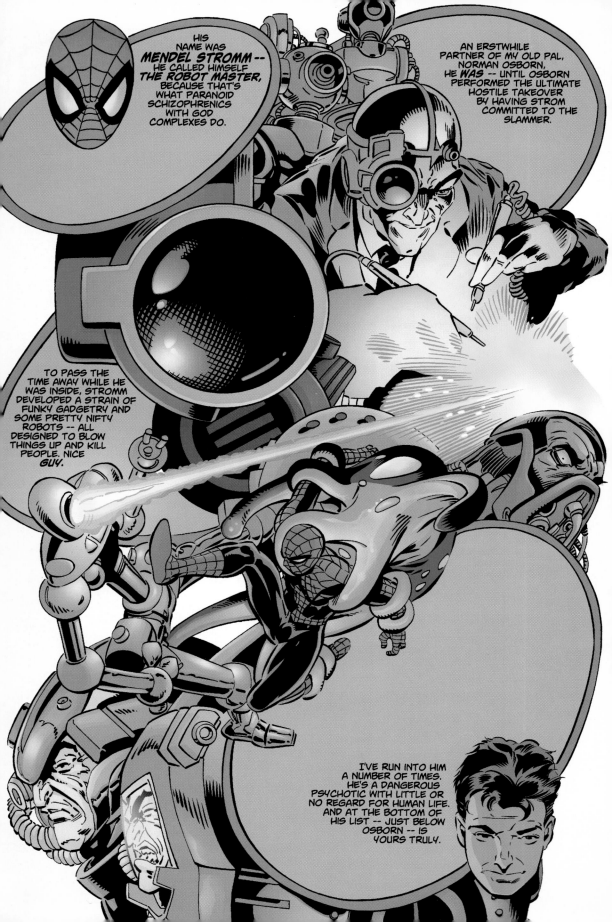

HIS NAME WAS **MENDEL STROMM** -- HE CALLED HIMSELF **THE ROBOT MASTER,** BECAUSE THAT'S WHAT PARANOID SCHIZOPHRENICS WITH GOD COMPLEXES DO.

AN ERSTWHILE PARTNER OF MY OLD PAL, NORMAN OSBORN, HE *WAS* -- UNTIL OSBORN PERFORMED THE ULTIMATE HOSTILE TAKEOVER BY HAVING STROM COMMITTED TO THE SLAMMER.

TO PASS THE TIME AWAY WHILE HE WAS INSIDE, STROMM DEVELOPED A STRAIN OF FUNKY GADGETRY AND SOME PRETTY NIFTY ROBOTS -- ALL DESIGNED TO BLOW THINGS UP AND KILL PEOPLE. NICE *GUY.*

I'VE RUN INTO HIM A NUMBER OF TIMES. HE'S A DANGEROUS PSYCHOTIC WITH LITTLE OR NO REGARD FOR HUMAN LIFE. AND AT THE BOTTOM OF HIS LIST -- JUST BELOW OSBORN -- IS YOURS TRULY.

"NATURALLY..."

KNOK
KNOK

NOW, *WHO* ON EARTH COULD THAT BE AT THIS TIME OF NIGHT--

-- OH, MY... IS THAT *YOU*, PETER?

HELLO, MISS SMITH.

WELL, WELL... A SIGNATURE VISIT FROM MY FAVORITE PUPIL. I WAS BEGINNING TO THINK YOU'D FORGOTTEN I *EXISTED.*

I'M NOT SURE IF THAT'S *POSSIBLE.* MY EARS ARE STILL RINGING FROM THE *LAST* TIME I SAW YOU.

DAPHNE SMITH -- AKA *"BOOMER"* -- WAS MY SCIENCE TEACHER IN TENTH GRADE, AND QUITE POSSIBLY THE KOOKIEST PERSON I EVER MET -- CERTAINLY ONE OF THE *SMARTEST*.

SHE WAS A TOTAL *NUT* -- THE ONE PERSON WHO COULD BRING AN ENTIRE CLASS TO ITS KNEES WITH LAUGHTER, WHILE AT THE SAME TIME HOLDING ITS INTEREST. SHE HAD A UNIQUE METHOD OF TEACHING, WHICH SHE CALLED *"CREATING A SPARK."*

"I COULD NEVER TELL IF THAT MEANT THE *FIGURATIVE* SPARK IN THE MINDS OF HER STUDENTS, OR IF IT REFERRED TO THE *HUGE* AND *DEAFENING EXPLOSIONS* THAT FREQUENTLY ROCKED HER CLASSROOM.

EITHER WAY, SHE *REALLY* KNEW HOW TO SHAKE THINGS UP. WHEN I WASN'T FEARING FOR MY SAFETY, I WAS TESTING THE COMBUSTIBILITY OF MY SURROUNDINGS IN NEW AND ALARMING WAYS.

SO, HOW HAVE YOU *BEEN*, MISS SMITH? BLOWN UP ANY FRESHMEN LATELY?

I'VE BEEN *WELL*, DEAR. MY, YOU *HAVE* FILLED OUT, HAVEN'T YOU? YOU USED TO BE SUCH A *SKINNY* LITTLE GEEK --

HEHH... *TOUCHÉ.* LISTEN, I WAS WONDERING IF YOU CAUGHT THE NEWS TONIGHT... ABOUT THOSE *ELECTRICAL SURGES* IN TIMES SQUARE?

I'M FREELANCING FOR THE BUGLE THESE DAYS AND I'VE BEEN TRYING MY HAND AT SOME ACTUAL REPORTING LATELY. I NEED TO BE *THOROUGH*--

AH, YES... THOSE CURIOUS SURGES. I DON'T KNOW IF YOU NOTICED, BUT THERE SHOULDN'T HAVE BEEN ANY SURGES *AT ALL*, PETER.

THE AVAILABLE MACHINERY SHOULDN'T HAVE BEEN ABLE TO CARRY THE NECESSARY *CURRENT*, FOR ONE THING.

YEAH... I NOTICED THAT. I ALSO NOTICED HOW THE ELECTRICAL EQUIPMENT REMAINED *INTACT*, DESPITE THE HIGH VOLTAGE THAT MUST'VE BEEN INVOLVED. IT SHOULD'VE BEEN *FRIED*.

GOOD BOY -- YOU ALWAYS WERE AS SHARP AS A *TACK*, MISTER PARKER. IF I WERE TRYING TO FIND OUT HOW SUCH A THING WERE POSSIBLE, I'D LOOK AT THE *SOURCE* FIRST.

THOSE SURGES OF ELECTRICITY HAD TO COME FROM *SOMEWHERE* ON THE GRID. I'D IMAGINE THE ELECTRICITY COMPANY IS TRYING TO PINPOINT IT AS WE SPEAK.

YEAH, OKAY.

LISTEN, UH... I DON'T KNOW IF YOU *HEARD* ABOUT MARY JANE--

I *DID* HEAR WHAT HAPPENED, MY LOVE, I'M SO SORRY ABOUT YOUR WIFE... SHE ALWAYS WAS SUCH A *SWEET* KID...

I KNOW YOU MUST MISS HER VERY MUCH.

YEAH, I DO. FUNNY THING IS, I FEEL LIKE SHE'S STILL *HERE*, YOU KNOW? I REALIZE IT'S JUST BECAUSE I *WANT* HER TO BE. ALL MY FRIENDS KEEP TELLING ME IT'S TIME TO LET GO.

BUT I DON'T *WANT* TO.

THEN *DON'T*.

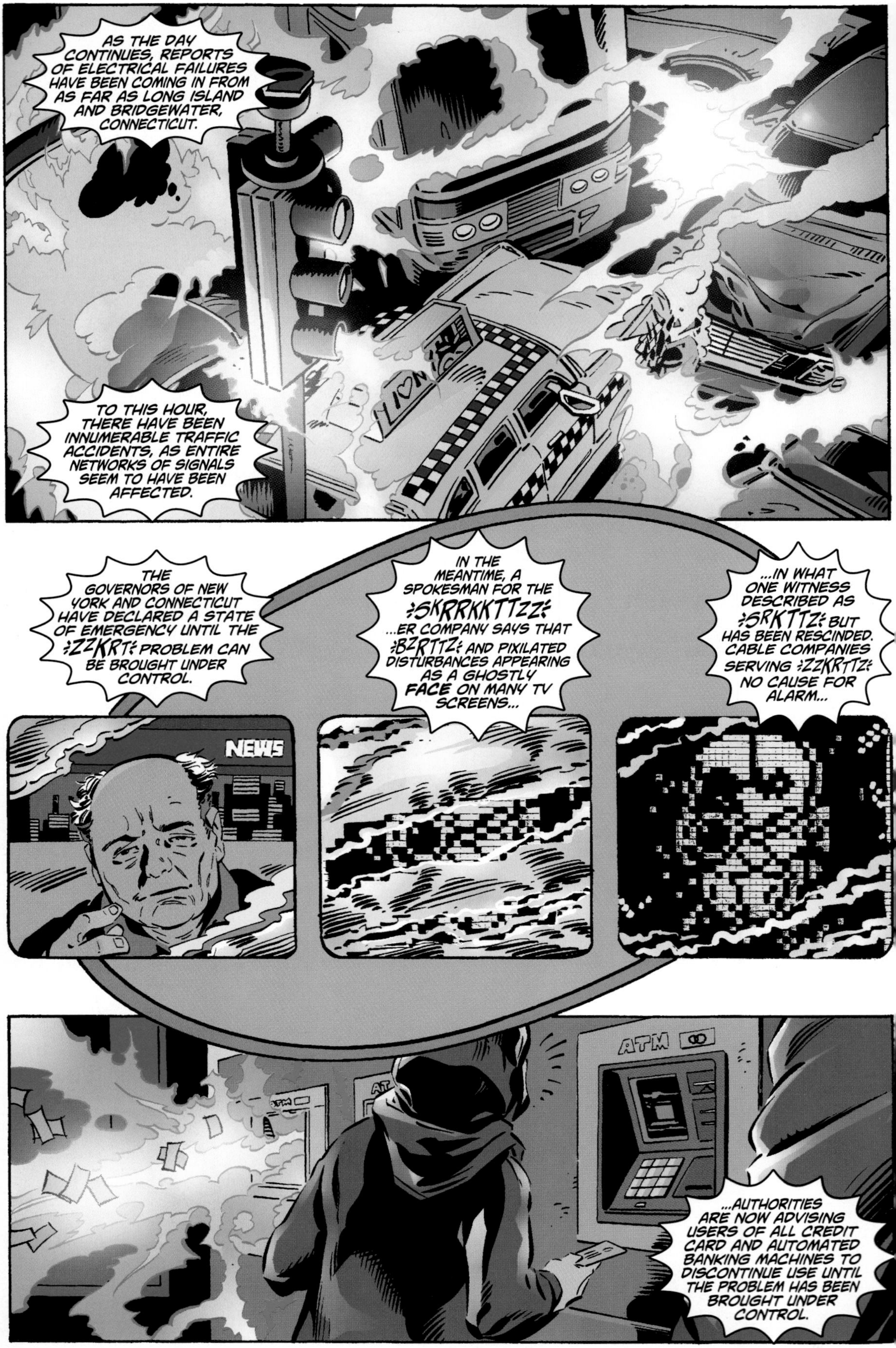
AS THE DAY CONTINUES, REPORTS OF ELECTRICAL FAILURES HAVE BEEN COMING IN FROM AS FAR AS LONG ISLAND AND BRIDGEWATER, CONNECTICUT.
TO THIS HOUR, THERE HAVE BEEN INNUMERABLE TRAFFIC ACCIDENTS, AS ENTIRE NETWORKS OF SIGNALS SEEM TO HAVE BEEN AFFECTED.
THE GOVERNORS OF NEW YORK AND CONNECTICUT HAVE DECLARED A STATE OF EMERGENCY UNTIL THE ZZKRT PROBLEM CAN BE BROUGHT UNDER CONTROL.
IN THE MEANTIME, A SPOKESMAN FOR THE SKRRKKTTZZ ...ER COMPANY SAYS THAT BZRTTZ AND PIXILATED DISTURBANCES APPEARING AS A GHOSTLY **FACE** ON MANY TV SCREENS...
...IN WHAT ONE WITNESS DESCRIBED AS SRKTTZ BUT HAS BEEN RESCINDED. CABLE COMPANIES SERVING ZZKRTTZ NO CAUSE FOR ALARM...
NEWS
ATM
...AUTHORITIES ARE NOW ADVISING USERS OF ALL CREDIT CARD AND AUTOMATED BANKING MACHINES TO DISCONTINUE USE UNTIL THE PROBLEM HAS BEEN BROUGHT UNDER CONTROL.

SO, THIS IS *LEGAL*... RIGHT, SHEA?

"*FREEDOM OF INFORMATION ACT*..." THAT'S ALL YOU NEED TO *KNOW*, DUDE.

BESIDES, THE WAY *I* SEE IT, YOU'RE JUST DOING YOUR CIVIC *DUTY*, RIGHT? AIN'T MY FAULT IF THE ELECTRIC COMPANY DON'T KNOW HOW TO PREVENT SOME INTERESTED THIRD PARTY FROM TAKING A LOOK AT THEIR LOCAL SERVER.

'*COURSE*, I SAID THAT WHEN THEY GOT ME FOR THE MICROSOFT HACK. I SHOULDA KEPT MY *MOUTH* SHUT, COME T'THINK OF IT...

ET VOILA! ONE ELECTRICAL GRID, MONSIEUR... AN' WOULD YOU LIKE *FRIES* WITH THAT?

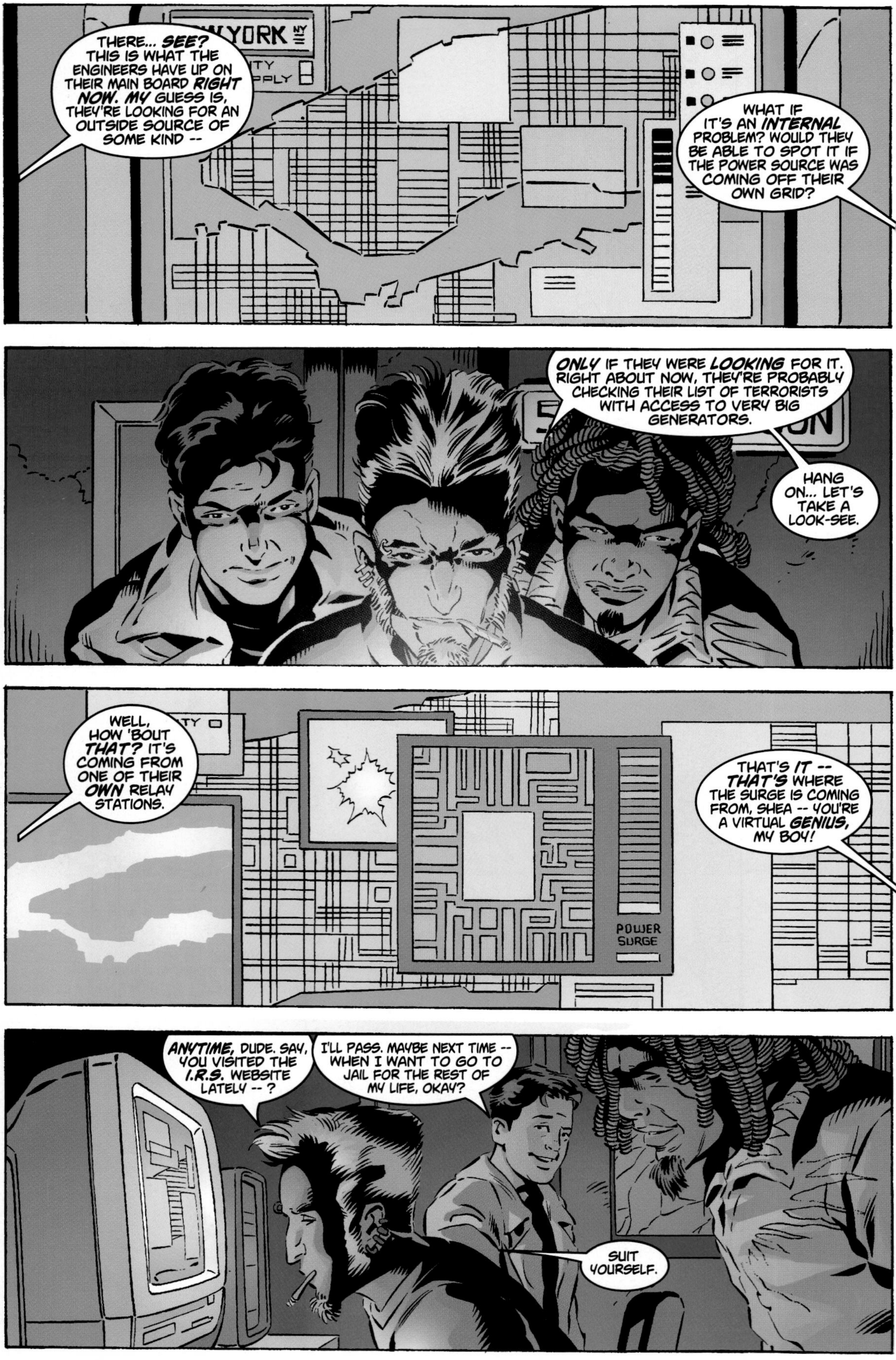
NEW YORK NY
THERE... SEE? THIS IS WHAT THE ENGINEERS HAVE UP ON THEIR MAIN BOARD RIGHT NOW. MY GUESS IS, THEY'RE LOOKING FOR AN OUTSIDE SOURCE OF SOME KIND --
WHAT IF IT'S AN INTERNAL PROBLEM? WOULD THEY BE ABLE TO SPOT IT IF THE POWER SOURCE WAS COMING OFF THEIR OWN GRID?
ONLY IF THEY WERE LOOKING FOR IT. RIGHT ABOUT NOW, THEY'RE PROBABLY CHECKING THEIR LIST OF TERRORISTS WITH ACCESS TO VERY BIG GENERATORS.
HANG ON... LET'S TAKE A LOOK-SEE.
WELL, HOW 'BOUT THAT? IT'S COMING FROM ONE OF THEIR OWN RELAY STATIONS.
POWER SURGE
THAT'S IT -- THAT'S WHERE THE SURGE IS COMING FROM, SHEA -- YOU'RE A VIRTUAL GENIUS, MY BOY!
ANYTIME, DUDE. SAY, YOU VISITED THE I.R.S. WEBSITE LATELY -- ?
I'LL PASS. MAYBE NEXT TIME -- WHEN I WANT TO GO TO JAIL FOR THE REST OF MY LIFE, OKAY?
SUIT YOURSELF.

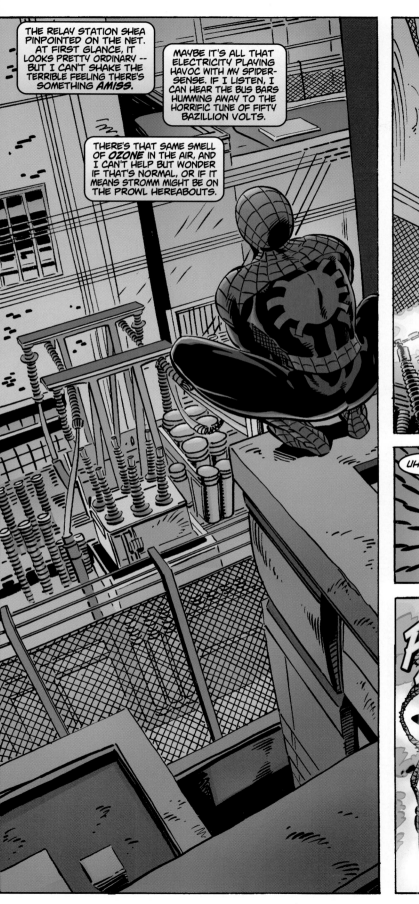

THE RELAY STATION SHEA PINPOINTED ON THE NET. AT FIRST GLANCE, IT LOOKS PRETTY ORDINARY -- BUT I CAN'T SHAKE THE TERRIBLE FEELING THERE'S SOMETHING *AMISS.*

MAYBE IT'S ALL THAT ELECTRICITY PLAYING HAVOC WITH MY SPIDER-SENSE. IF I LISTEN, I CAN HEAR THE BUS BARS HUMMING AWAY TO THE HORRIFIC TUNE OF FIFTY BAZILLION VOLTS.

THERE'S THAT SAME SMELL OF *OZONE* IN THE AIR, AND I CAN'T HELP BUT WONDER IF THAT'S NORMAL, OR IF IT MEANS STROMM MIGHT BE ON THE PROWL HEREABOUTS.

I REALLY SHOULD HAVE PAID ATTENTION IN BOOMER'S SCIENCE CLASS INSTEAD OF MAKING ALL THOSE *EXPLOSIONS* --

UH-OH.

FZZAK

OW! JEEZ... THEY'RE *EVERYWHERE.* I GOTTA FIND SOME --

ZZZAAAKK

--COVER!

CRASH!

UHH..!

SCIENCE WHIZ OR NOT, ONE THING IS CLEAR: I HAVE ABOUT TEN SECONDS BEFORE STROMM'S NEW ELECTRICAL TOYS BREAK IN AND TURN ME INTO SPIDER *FRICASSEE.*

AND THE ONLY WAY OUT SEEMS TO BE *DOWN.*

WELL WELL, ROBOT MASTER... HAVEN'T YOU BEEN A BUSY *BOY* --

♪ YOO-HOO! ANYBODY HOME? MENDEL? ♪ IT'S ME, YOUR FRIENDLY NEIGHBORHOOD SANTY CLAUS!

THE GOOFY BANTER IS AS MUCH TO COMFORT *MYSELF* AS TO ENGAGE IN ANY ACTUAL CONVERSATION. IF STROMM DID ANSWER ME AT A TIME LIKE THIS, I'D PROBABLY *FREAK*.

I CAN'T HELP THINKING HOW IF THERE'S A WHITE RABBIT WITH A POCKET WATCH WAITING FOR ME AT THE BOTTOM OF THIS HOLE, I'M *DEFINITELY* GOING TO RETIRE.

THE TUNNEL EXTENDS AS FAR AS I CAN SEE. STRANGE... EVEN THOUGH MY SPIDER-SENSE IS STILL SCREAMING AT ME LIKE RATS PLAYING A VIOLIN, I *STILL* CAN'T SEE WHAT'S WRONG.

I DON'T FEEL STROMM'S PRESENCE AT ALL. IT'S THESE WEIRD CABLES -- THEY SEEM TO BE ORGANIC... ALMOST *ALIV--*

GAH!

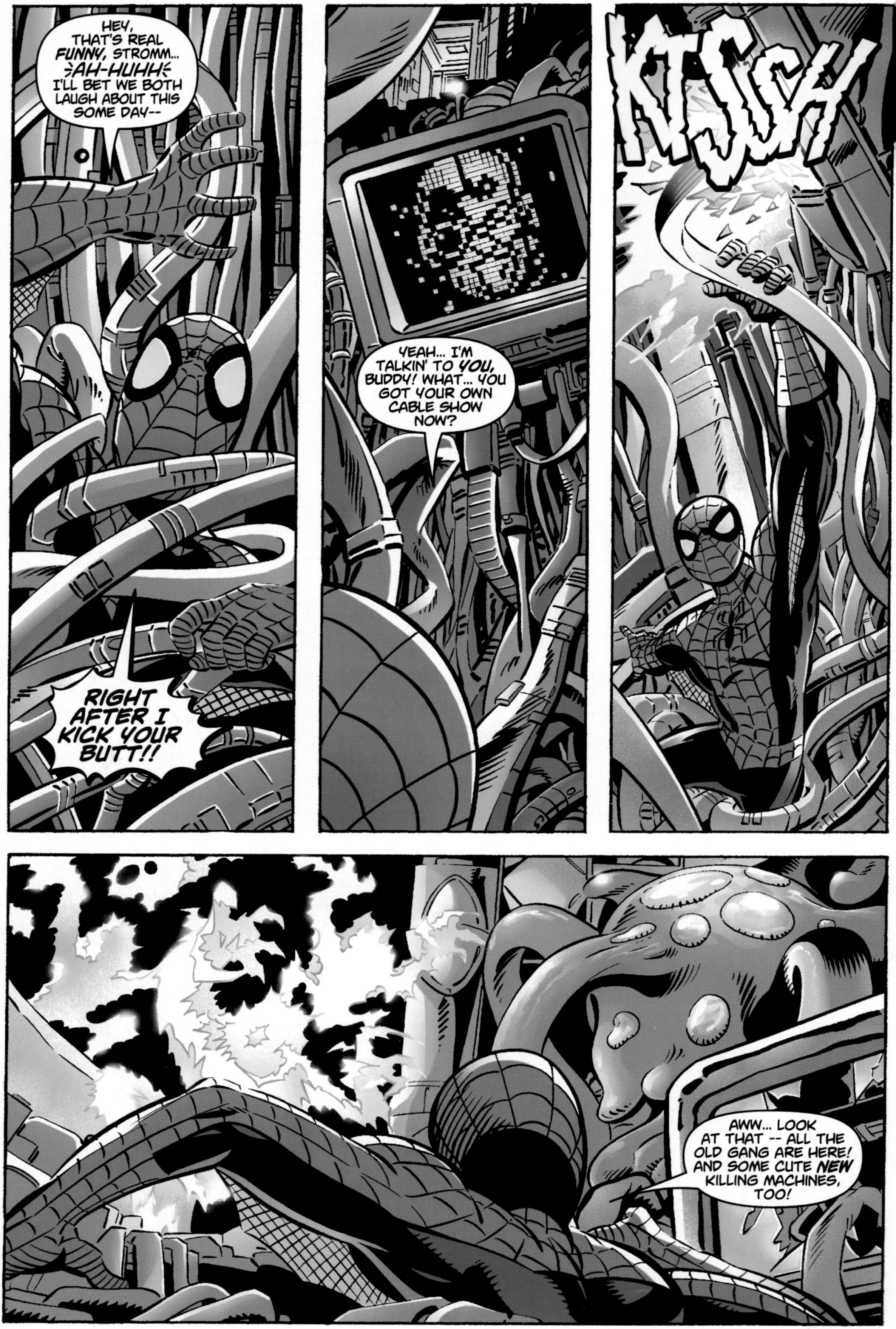
HEY, THAT'S REAL FUNNY, STROMM... AH-HUHH I'LL BET WE BOTH LAUGH ABOUT THIS SOME DAY--
RIGHT AFTER I KICK YOUR BUTT!!
YEAH... I'M TALKIN' TO YOU, BUDDY! WHAT... YOU GOT YOUR OWN CABLE SHOW NOW?
KTSSCH
AWW... LOOK AT THAT -- ALL THE OLD GANG ARE HERE! AND SOME CUTE NEW KILLING MACHINES, TOO!

I'LL TELL YOU THIS, STROMM...;HUFF..!; YOU BETTER...

YOU BETTER'VE BEEN PRACTICING YOUR *KUNG FU*, OR SOMETHIN'. 'CAUSE WHEN I GET TO WHEREVER YOU ARE, I'M GONNA MAKE YOU EAT EVERY SINGLE *ONE* OF THESE BLASTED ROBOTS.

HH-AHH!, ;HUFF..!; *GANGWAY!* TALLY *HO!*

OKAY, ROBOT MASTER... WHAT SAY WE MAKE THIS BETWEEN YOU AND ME, FACE TO--

--FACE..?

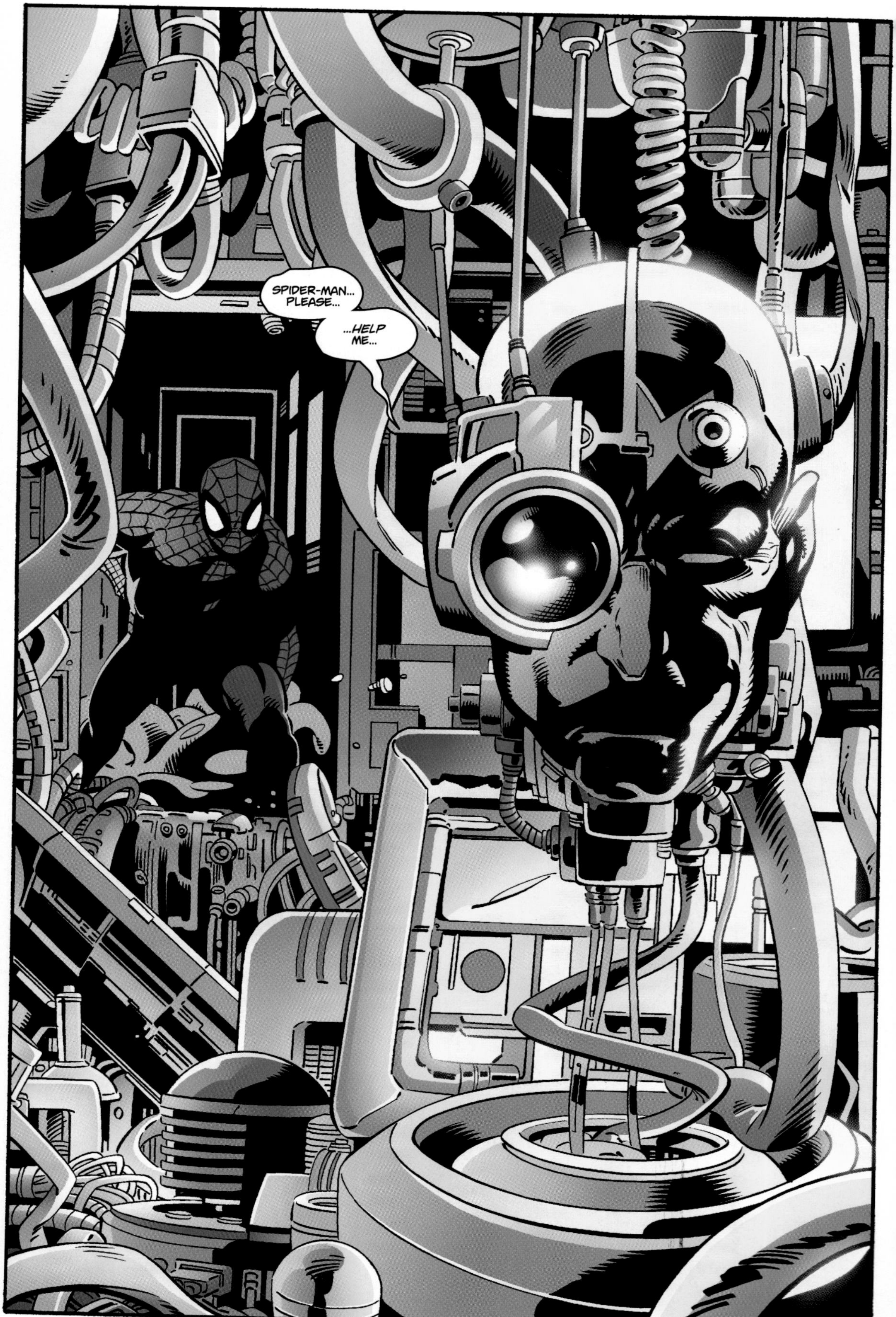
SPIDER-MAN... PLEASE...
...HELP ME...

SOME PEOPLE TAKE THINGS TOO *SERIOUSLY*, IF YOU ASK ME.

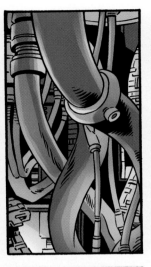

I MEAN, ME, I'VE NEVER BEEN ONE FOR THE DAILY *GRIND*... I'M MORE OF YOUR *FREELANCE* TYPE, EVEN IF IT *DOES* PAY PEANUT SHELLS, OF WHICH THE IRS TAKES FIFTY PERCENT.

BUT *SOME* PEOPLE... IT'S LIKE THEY'RE MARRIED TO *MISERY*. THEY HATE THEIR JOBS FROM THE MOMENT THEY FIRST CLOCK IN, BUT FIGURE THEY'LL JUST STICK IT OUT A WHILE UNTIL SOMETHING BETTER COMES ALONG, RIGHT?

ONLY, BEFORE THEY KNOW WHAT'S HAPPENED, THERE'S A MORTGAGE AND TWO-POINT-FIVE KIDS AND PLANS FOR A SAILBOAT AND A PENSION PLAN. AND THEY CAN'T GET *OUT*.

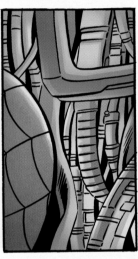

THAT MUST REALLY BE DEPRESSING: TO BE STUCK IN A DEAD-END JOB YOU HATE, TRUDGING THROUGH A LIFE YOU HATE EVEN WORSE. LIVING PAYCHECK TO PAYCHECK WITHOUT THE GUTS TO MOVE ON.

I GUESS THERE'S A MORAL IN THERE SOMEWHERE: YOU HAVE TO LEARN TO DISTANCE YOURSELF FROM YOUR WORK...

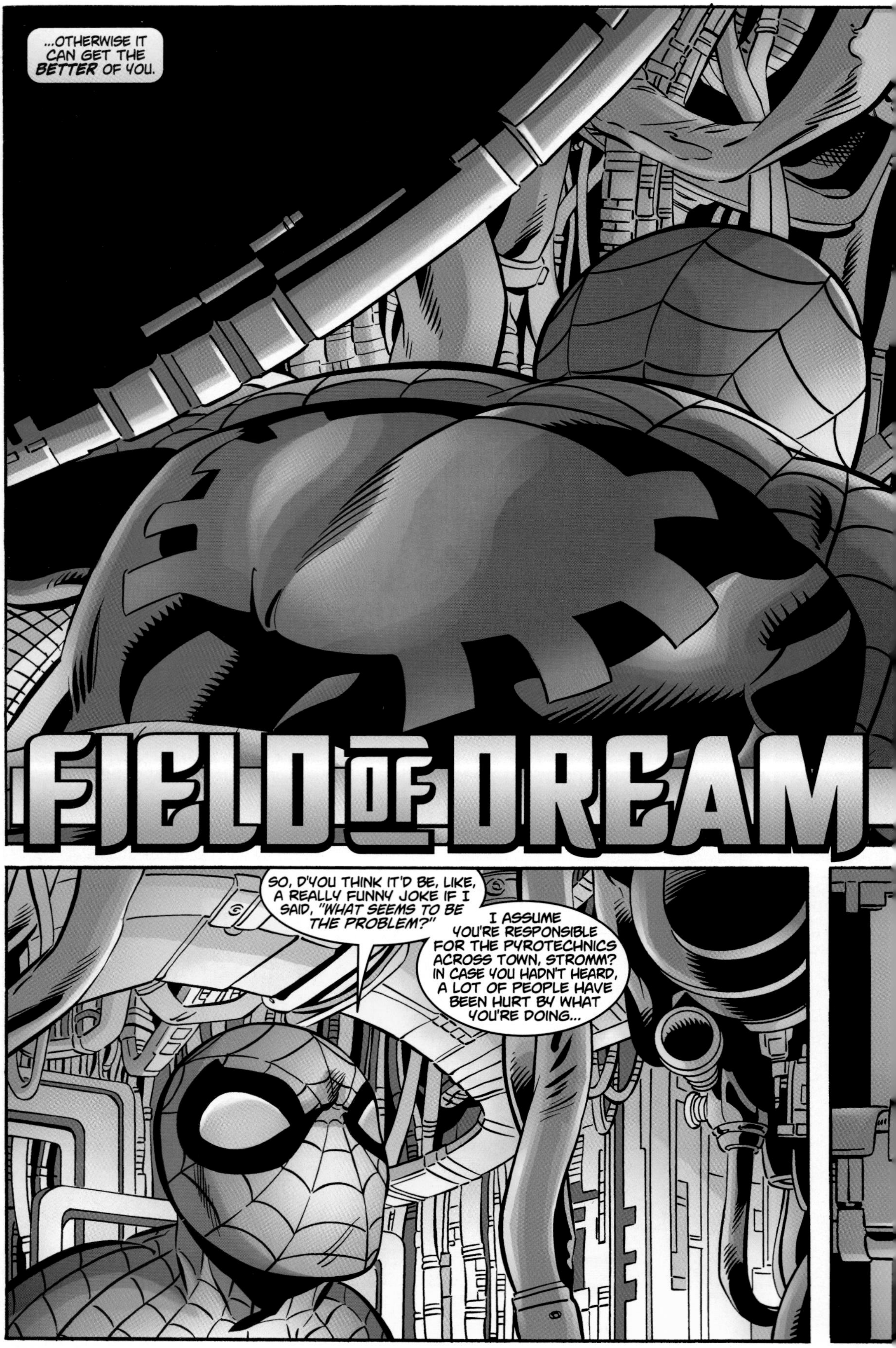
...OTHERWISE IT CAN GET THE BETTER OF YOU.
FIELD OF DREAM
SO, D'YOU THINK IT'D BE, LIKE, A REALLY FUNNY JOKE IF I SAID, "WHAT SEEMS TO BE THE PROBLEM?"
I ASSUME YOU'RE RESPONSIBLE FOR THE PYROTECHNICS ACROSS TOWN, STROMM? IN CASE YOU HADN'T HEARD, A LOT OF PEOPLE HAVE BEEN HURT BY WHAT YOU'RE DOING...

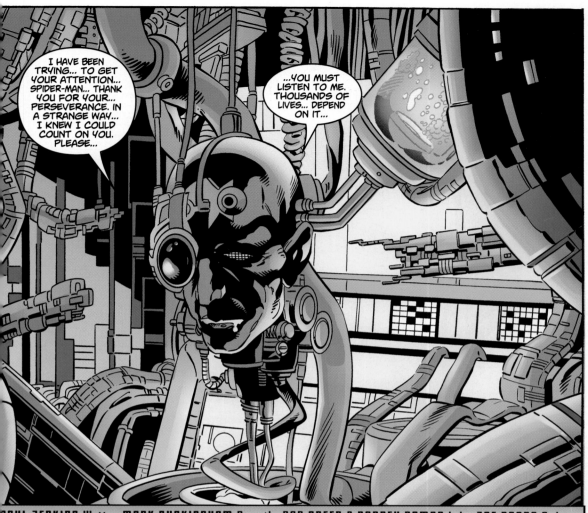

I HAVE BEEN TRYING... TO GET YOUR ATTENTION... SPIDER-MAN... THANK YOU FOR YOUR... PERSEVERANCE. IN A STRANGE WAY... I KNEW I COULD COUNT ON YOU. PLEASE...

...YOU MUST LISTEN TO ME. THOUSANDS OF LIVES... DEPEND ON IT...

PAUL JENKINS Writer MARK BUCKINGHAM Pencils DAN GREEN & RODNEY RAMOS Inks JOE ROSAS Colors RICHARD STARKINGS & COMICRAFT Letters AXEL ALONSO Editor JOE QUESADA Editor in Chief

YOU DON'T UNDERSTAND, SPIDER-MAN... WHERE ONCE I WAS THE ROBOT MASTER... I AM NOW MERELY ITS SERVANT...

THIS RECENT UPHEAVAL... THE SURGES IN THE ELECTRICAL GRID -- NONE OF THIS IS MY DOING...

...IT IS THE WORK OF THE MACHINE.

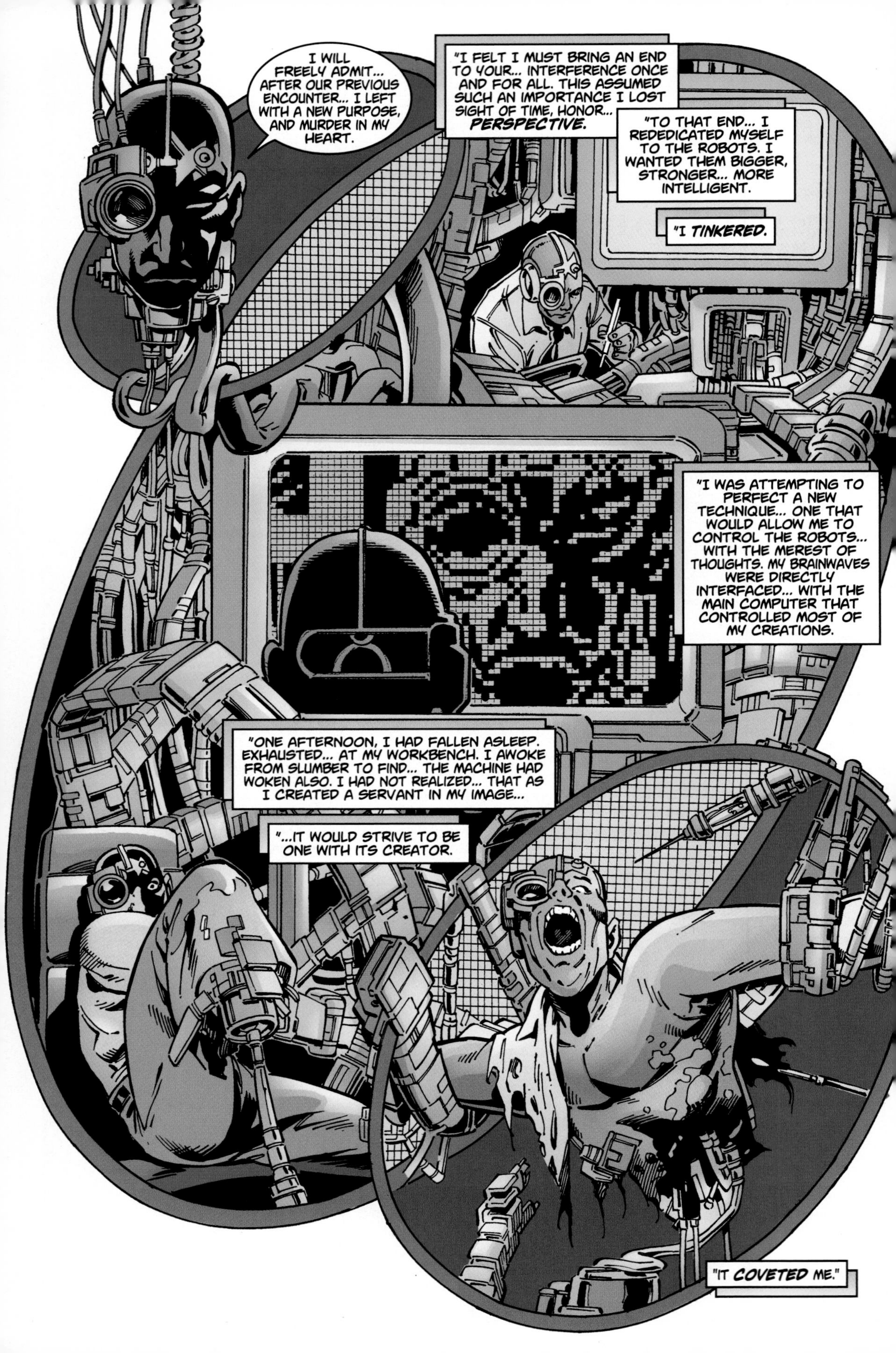
I WILL FREELY ADMIT... AFTER OUR PREVIOUS ENCOUNTER... I LEFT WITH A NEW PURPOSE, AND MURDER IN MY HEART.
"I FELT I MUST BRING AN END TO YOUR... INTERFERENCE ONCE AND FOR ALL. THIS ASSUMED SUCH AN IMPORTANCE I LOST SIGHT OF TIME, HONOR... PERSPECTIVE.
"TO THAT END... I REDEDICATED MYSELF TO THE ROBOTS. I WANTED THEM BIGGER, STRONGER... MORE INTELLIGENT.
"I TINKERED.
"I WAS ATTEMPTING TO PERFECT A NEW TECHNIQUE... ONE THAT WOULD ALLOW ME TO CONTROL THE ROBOTS... WITH THE MEREST OF THOUGHTS. MY BRAINWAVES WERE DIRECTLY INTERFACED... WITH THE MAIN COMPUTER THAT CONTROLLED MOST OF MY CREATIONS.
"ONE AFTERNOON, I HAD FALLEN ASLEEP. EXHAUSTED... AT MY WORKBENCH. I AWOKE FROM SLUMBER TO FIND... THE MACHINE HAD WOKEN ALSO. I HAD NOT REALIZED... THAT AS I CREATED A SERVANT IN MY IMAGE...
"...IT WOULD STRIVE TO BE ONE WITH ITS CREATOR.
"IT COVETED ME."

THE MACHINE HAS BECOME ALIVE, SPIDER-MAN. WITH IT... I SHARE A MEASURE OF CONTROL. BUT THE POWER STRUCTURE IS EPHEMERAL... ILL-DEFINED AT BEST.

FOR THE MOMENT, I AM STRONGER... BUT WITH EVERY PASSING MOMENT, THE MACHINE GAINS INFLUENCE.

SO, WHAT'M I SUPPOSED TO DO? I WAS HOPING TO HAVE BEEN PUNCHING SOMEONE BY NOW.

I KNOW YOU, SPIDER-MAN... DESPITE OUR PAST DIFFERENCES AND YOUR GLIB APPROACH TO MATTERS OF IMPORTANCE... YOU ARE NOT A STUPID MAN.

YOU MUST UNDERSTAND... THE PAIN IS UNBEARABLE. I FEEL THAT I AM... MERE MOMENTS AWAY... FROM BEING OVERWHELMED.

THE MACHINE ATTACKS ME FROM ALL FRONTS... IT GRATES AT MY NERVE ENDINGS. IF I LOSE CONTROL... IT WILL ATTEMPT TO REPRODUCE. AND IN SO DOING... IT WILL OVERRUN THE ENTIRE NETWORK.

THE KEY IS YOU, SPIDER-MAN... IT IS NOW A QUESTION OF CHOICE, AND A GRAVE CHOICE IT IS.

I SUSPECT YOU ALREADY KNOW... THAT THERE IS ONLY ONE SOLUTION TO THIS PROBLEM:

PLEASE... IF YOU HAVE ANY MERCY INSIDE YOU...

...KILL ME.

PLEASE, GOD... KILL ME NOW.

MM? WHAT DID YOU SAY, HON?

MM? OH, I WAS JUST SAYING I LIKED THE RED ONES BETTER. UH... THAN THE GREEN ONES, I MEAN.

RANDY! YOU SAID YOU LIKED THE GREEN ONES BETTER BEFORE. I THOUGHT YOU *LIKED* SPENDING TIME WITH ME --

IT'S NOTHING LIKE THAT, GLORY. I PROMISE. IT'S JUST... I TOLD PETE I'D GO HANG OUT WITH HIM AND WATCH THE KNICKS GAME TONIGHT.

I MEAN, YOU KNOW... HE'S BEEN THROUGH SUCH A TOUGH TIME LATELY, WHAT WITH MARY JANE AND ALL. I JUST WANTED TO MAKE SURE HE'S OKAY --

RANDY ROBERTSON, MAY GOD STRIKE ME DEAD IF THERE ISN'T ACTUALLY A SWEET, CARING BOY UNDERNEATH THAT PARTY-HOUND EXTERIOR OF YOURS.

AND HERE I WAS THINKING YOU WERE JUST GETTING BORED.

WELL, DON'T YOU WORRY ABOUT PETER, HONEYBUN, HE'S ALWAYS BEEN ONE TO DEAL WITH THINGS ON HIS OWN. BESIDES, HE HAS A LOT BETTER THINGS TO DO THAN GO SHOE SHOPPING WITH YOU AN' ME...

NICE TRY, SON.

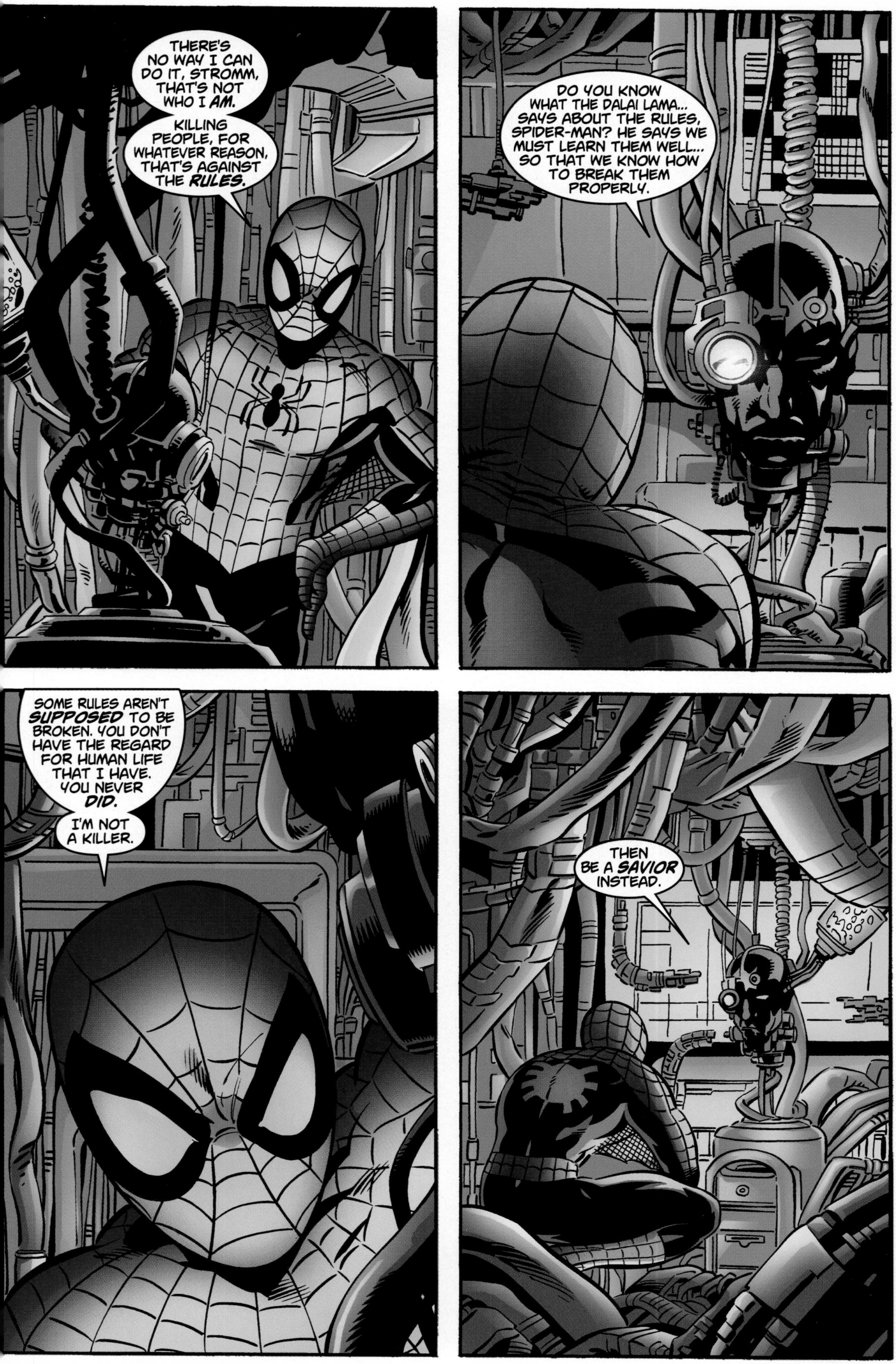
THERE'S NO WAY I CAN DO IT, STROMM, THAT'S NOT WHO I AM.
KILLING PEOPLE, FOR WHATEVER REASON, THAT'S AGAINST THE RULES.
DO YOU KNOW WHAT THE DALAI LAMA... SAYS ABOUT THE RULES, SPIDER-MAN? HE SAYS WE MUST LEARN THEM WELL... SO THAT WE KNOW HOW TO BREAK THEM PROPERLY.
SOME RULES AREN'T SUPPOSED TO BE BROKEN. YOU DON'T HAVE THE REGARD FOR HUMAN LIFE THAT I HAVE. YOU NEVER DID.
I'M NOT A KILLER.
THEN BE A SAVIOR INSTEAD.

ASK YOURSELF... IS A SACRIFICE A SUICIDE? IS IT MURDER WHEN THE ACTION OF MURDER... WILL SAVE A THOUSAND OTHERS?

THE MACHINE IS GOING TO ASSUME CONTROL... IT IS *INEVITABLE,* SPIDER-MAN... WHETHER YOU CARE TO ACCEPT IT OR NOT. WHEN THAT HAPPENS...I WILL BE SUBJECTED TO TORTURES UNDREAMED OF FOR AS LONG AS THE MACHINE REMAINS ALIVE.

AND WHAT THEN...? WHAT ABOUT HOSPITAL MACHINERY... AIR TRAFFIC CONTROL... PRISON COMPUTERS...?

READJUST YOUR... PRIORITIES, SPIDER-MAN. RE-EVALUATE YOUR VALUES. A THOUSAND PEOPLE ARE GOING TO DIE... IN THE NAME OF YOUR MORALITY.

ASK YOURSELF IF YOU'RE WILLING... TO TAKE RESPONSIBILITY FOR THEM *ALL.*

AND SO, AS THE SITUATION WORSENS... KZZZ... AUTHORITIES ARE UNABLE TO EXPLAIN...KZZ

IN FACT, AS... KZZZ... AND THE KZSHH

CLICK

TCH... I NEVER *DID* LIKE THIS CONTRAPTION. YOU CAN'T GET A DECENT RECEPTION NOWADAYS-- I THINK IT'S ALL THESE CHANNELS THEY KEEP ADDING...

HELLO? ARE YOU WITH US, MISTER PARKER? PETER?

PETER, DEAR...?

MM? OH, SORRY, AUNT MAY... I WAS JUST, UH... THINKING ABOUT SOMETHING.

AUNT MAY, I NEED TO ASK YOU A QUESTION, OKAY? I WANT YOU TO BE TOTALLY HONEST WITH ME.

LET'S SAY YOU GOT REALLY SICK ONE DAY. MAYBE IF YOU WERE DYING AND IN A LOT OF PAIN--

I WOULDN'T ASK THAT QUESTION IF I WERE YOU, PETER-- YOU MAY NOT LIKE THE ANSWER.

I CAN DEAL WITH WHATEVER YOU SAY, AUNT MAY-- I PROMISE. I JUST... I REALLY HAVE TO *KNOW*, OKAY?

-:SIGH:- I SUPPOSE THIS WAS ALWAYS GOING TO COME UP BETWEEN US ONE OF THESE DAYS. VERY WELL, THEN...

I'M GOING TO TELL YOU A STORY, PETER-- IT'S SOMETHING I'VE NEVER SHARED WITH ANYONE, NOT EVEN YOUR UNCLE BEN. IT MAY NOT ANSWER YOUR QUESTION, BUT PERHAPS THERE IS NO ANSWER.

"IT HAPPENED WHEN I WAS JUST A LITTLE GIRL... I COULDN'T HAVE BEEN MORE THAN FIVE OR SIX YEARS OLD AT THE TIME. I WAS A VERY PENSIVE LITTLE THING... SO QUIET AND SENSITIVE.

"MY FATHER'S OLDER BROTHER, HORACE, HAD BEEN TAKEN DEATHLY ILL.

"I DIDN'T KNOW IT AT THE TIME, BUT HE'D BEEN STRICKEN WITH *CANCER*. THE FAMILY TRIED TO HIDE IT FROM ME IN CASE IT SCARED ME.

"INTUITIVELY, I WANTED TO COMFORT HIM. I SNUCK INTO HIS ROOM ONE AFTERNOON...

"...UNCLE HORACE HAD ALWAYS BEEN SUCH A KIND MAN -- LARGER THAN LIFE AND AS STRONG AS AN OX. BUT TOWARDS THE END, THE POOR SOUL DIDN'T SEEM LIKE THE SAME PERSON AT ALL..."

M-MAY... IS THAT YOU, CHILD...?

OHH... MAY... IT HURTS...

I'M SO SORRY...

UNCLE HORACE NEEDS TO REST NOW, MAYFLY-- YOU MUSTN'T DISTURB HIM.

COME ON.

WHY'S HE CRYIN', DADDY?

THAT NIGHT, MY UNCLE HORACE TOOK HIS OWN LIFE WITH A REVOLVER.

I LOVED HIM AN AWFUL LOT... THAT HE WAS GONE SO SUDDENLY, I DIDN'T UNDERSTAND IT. I THOUGHT HE'D GONE TO VISIT SOMEONE AND THAT HE'D BE BACK THE FOLLOWING WEEK.

"I REMEMBER AFTER THE CORONER LEFT, MY FATHER STOOD OUT ON THE PORCH, ALL ALONE. IT WAS A VERY COLD NIGHT, BUT HE DIDN'T SEEM TO CARE. HE JUST STOOD THERE."

DADDY --

GO BACK INSIDE, MAYFLY.

PLEASE... GO BACK INSIDE...

"EVEN THOUGH I WAS SO YOUNG, I KNEW IN MY HEART WHAT MUST HAVE HAPPENED AND I'VE KEPT IT A SECRET UNTIL THIS DAY. YOU SEE, UNCLE HORACE HADN'T *OWNED* A REVOLVER."

WELL... -:SNFF...:- THAT WAS ALL SUCH A LONG TIME AGO. I'M SURE IT DOESN'T REALLY MATTER ANYMORE, DEAR.

GOD, I SWEAR, I'VE NEVER SEEN HIM THIS INTENSE. WHAT D'YOU THINK HE'S UP TO, SHEA?

I DUNNO -- HE JUS' GOT ALL INDUSTRIOUS AND SAID HE WANTED SOME PRIVACY FOR A WHILE.

HE'S PROBABLY IN A CHATROOM CALLIN' HIMSELF "LOVEMONKEY" AND TRYIN' TO PERSUADE SOME INTERNET CHICK HE'S A MERCHANT BANKER...

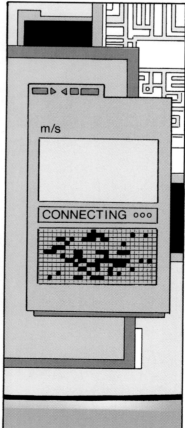

m/s

CONNECTING ooo

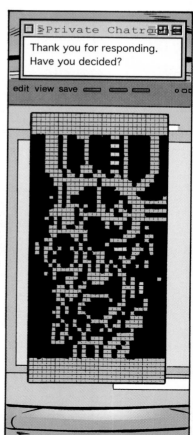

Private Chatroom

Thank you for responding. Have you decided?

edit view save

Please. The pain is intolerable. Time is of the essence. Have you decided?

Yes.

You are going to help me? As I suggested?

Yes.

Thank you, Spider-Man. Very well, then... let us discuss procedure.

I am currently uploading to your computer a copy of the operating system that my former neural network has now become. You must find a way to introduce a virus into this program and install it back here at the source.

Be advised, the machine will do everything in its power to stop you. It is aware of our communication and is at this very moment attempting to sever the connection between us.

The virus must be capable of utterly wiping the system, thus destroying both myself and the machine. Are you capable of creating such a virus?

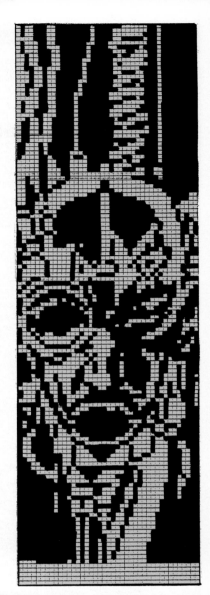

I think I know someone who can help. Give me a couple of hours.

...ealize this must have ...en a very difficult ...cision for you. Thank ...u for allowing me to ... with dignity.

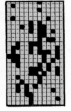

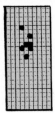

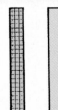

HEY, SHEA! CAN YOU GIVE ME A SECOND OVER HERE?

YOU REMEMBER I ASKED YOU ABOUT COMPUTER OPERATING SYSTEMS? LIKE, IF I GAVE YOU THE PROGRAM, WOULD YOU KNOW HOW TO *DISABLE* IT?

MADISON

DUDE, IT'S A LITTLE-KNOWN FACT I INVENTED MOST OPERATING SYSTEMS IN MY FORMER LIFE.

SO, YOU REALLY WANNA TAKE OUT SOMEONE'S HARD DRIVE, HUH? DO MY EARS DECEIVE ME, OR IS *"MISTER CLEAN-CUT"* ABOUT TO COMMIT AN ACT OF CYBER *TERRORISM?*

YOU KNOW WHAT I *WANT*. CAN YOU *DO* IT?

YEAH... I MEAN, DON'T TELL ANYONE I SAID THIS, BUT COMPUTER VIRUSES ARE MY SPECIALITY.

WELCOME TO THE WIPEOUT CLUB, MISTER PARKER.

BY THE TIME I GET BACK TO THE ROBOT MASTER'S RELAY STATION. SOMETHING IS RADICALLY *DIFFERENT* THAN BEFORE.

CALL IT A HUNCH, CALL IT SPIDER-SENSE, CALL IT A HERO'S INTUITION... I DON'T KNOW. I CAN SENSE THE MACHINE ALL AROUND... BUT IT'S LAYING LOW FOR SOME REASON.

INSIDE, EVERYTHING'S QUIETER THAN THE FIRST TIME I CAME HERE -- *TOO* QUIET. THE ARCING ELECTRICITY HAS BEEN REPLACED WITH A QUIET HUMMING...THERE'S ABSOLUTELY NO MOVEMENT.

IT DOESN'T REALLY SMELL LIKE OZONE ANYMORE-- IT SMELLS LIKE TROUBLE. THERE'S DEFINITELY SOMETHING DOWN THERE.

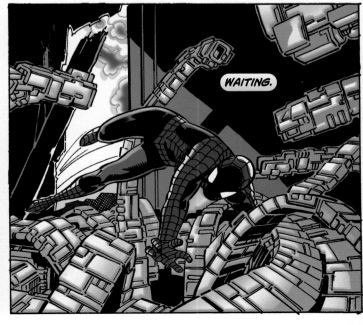

WAITING.

YOO HOO! IT'S ME AGAIN!

UM. OKAY... ANY CRAZED MACHINERY, HOMICIDAL ROBOTS AND/OR PSYCHOTIC CAN OPENERS PLEASE MAKE THEMSELVES KNOWN.

YES? NO? ANYONE?

WELL, NOW. SOMETHING TELLS ME YOU'RE NOT THE JANITOR.

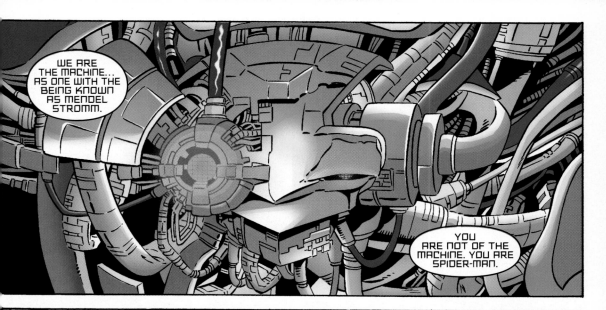

WE ARE THE MACHINE... AS ONE WITH THE BEING KNOWN AS MENDEL STROMM.

YOU ARE NOT OF THE MACHINE. YOU ARE SPIDER-MAN.

YOU WILL BE ELIMINATED.

SOMETIMES, I WONDER IF THAT OLD SPIDER-SENSE OF MINE ISN'T REALLY JUST DEJA VU...

DID YOU EVER SEE THAT MOVIE, "THE FORBIN PROJECT" WHERE THIS GUY INVENTS THIS COMPUTER THAT TAKES OVER THE ENTIRE WORLD?

SEE, HE DOESN'T REALIZE WHAT HE'S DONE. HE THINKS HIS MACHINE IS GOING TO BENEFIT MANKIND AND IT ENDS UP GOING LOOPY AND TAKING CHARGE.

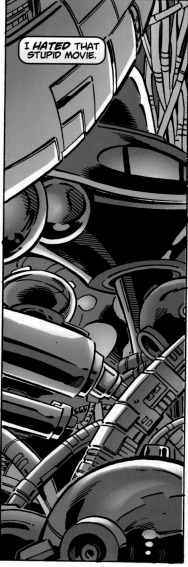

I HATED THAT STUPID MOVIE.

NN-AAHH!

KER-RUNCH!

...HHH...SORRY TO DISAPPOINT, OLD CHAP... BUT I HAVE AN APPOINTMENT WITH YOUR BOSS. CAN YOU FETCH US SOME COFFEE AND DONUTS, THERE'S A GOOD ROBOT...?

NO! YOU ARE DENIED ACCESS! DO NOT PROCEED!

ACCESS DENIED! ACCESS DENIED!

WHOOSH

THERE -- UP AHEAD. WITH ANY LUCK, HE'S STILL IN ONE PIECE...

STROMM? YOU STILL THERE?

MENDEL...?

SPIDER-MAN... PLEASE...)ZZTT(... I FEAR THAT IT IS NOW... OR NEVER...

...I AM OVERCOME... THE PAIN...)ZZTT(... THE MACHINE LIVES...

YEAH, WELL... NOT FOR LONG!

CHUNK

STOP! NO! YOU ARE DENIED ACCESS!

WHAT ARE YOU...

...DDD-OOOO-IIII-NNN-GGG??

I *COULDN'T* DO IT, MENDEL. I MEAN, I BEAT MYSELF UP OVER THIS LIKE YOU WOULDN'T BELIEVE. I MUST'VE THOUGHT ABOUT IT A THOUSAND DIFFERENT WAYS...

...BUT IT'S JUST NOT *ME*.

I TOLD MY COMPUTER BUDDY WE WERE PLAYING A PRACTICAL JOKE ON SOMEONE, SO I HAD HIM CREATE SOME KIND OF *LOOP PROGRAM* FOR YOU.

YOU'RE GOING TO BE ON *STANDBY* UNTIL I CAN WORK OUT JUST HOW TO GET YOU OUT OF THIS MESS. AND I WON'T REST UNTIL THAT HAPPENS, OKAY?

I'LL COME BACK FOR YOU, STROMM... I PROMISE.

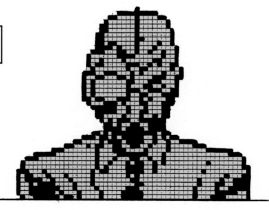

"IN THE MEANTIME, YOU HAVE A GOOD *SLEEP*, MAN..."

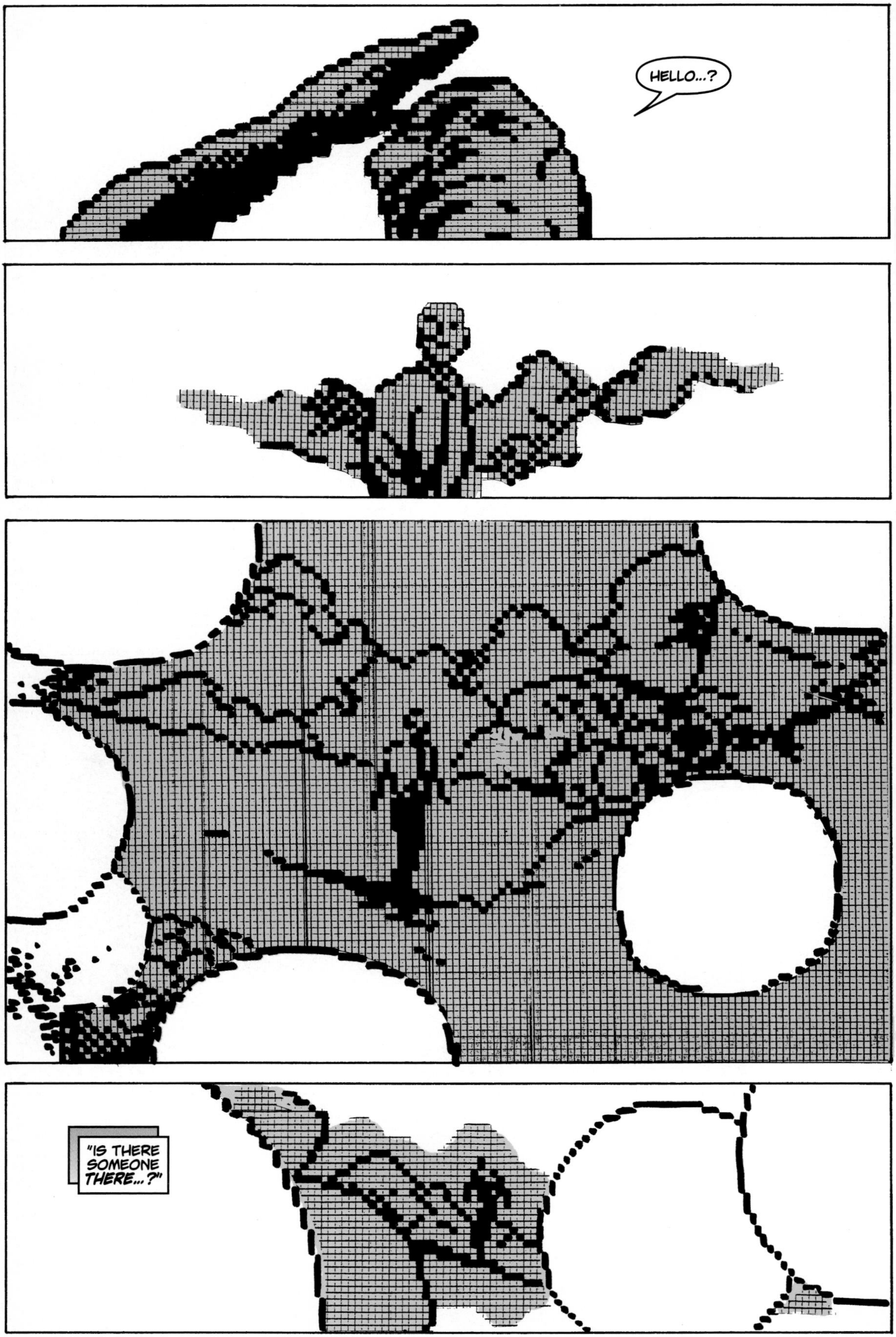
HELLO...?
"IS THERE SOMEONE THERE...?"

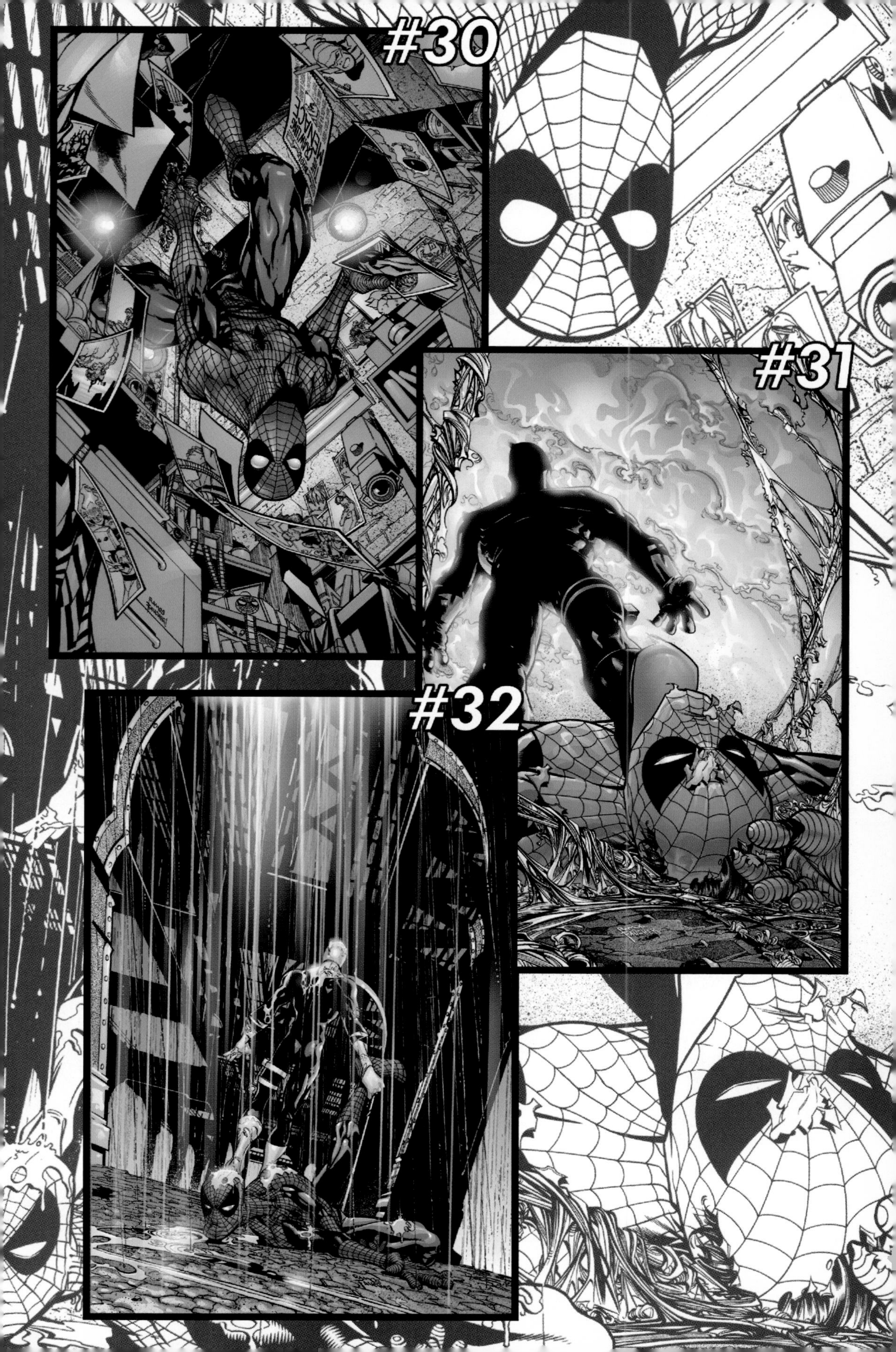
#30
#31
#32

THREE HUNDRED.

THREE HUNDRED? WHAT GAME IS *HE* PLAYING?

DUDE, THREE *HUNDRED?* ARE YOU SERIOUS?

THE QUESTION IS: "HOW MANY HOME RUNS DID BABE RUTH HIT DURING THE 1927 SEASON?"

I DUNNO... FOUR? *FIVE?*

PETER, HON, EVEN *I* KNOW BABE RUTH HIT *SIXTY*... AN' YOU COULDN'T *PAY* ME TO SIT THROUGH A BALL GAME.

YEAH, WELL... I'M NOT MUCH OF A BASEBALL FAN. I MEAN, *YOU* KNOW -- SOME GUY HITS A FEW HOMERS, SOME GUNG HO DESPERADO BUYS THE BALLS FOR, LIKE TWELVE BILLION BUCKS.

I GOTTA GET A DRINK, OKAY?

JEEZ... WHAT'S EATING *HIM?*

SO, UH... THIS "GROOVY LITTLE PAD" THING YOU GOT GOIN' HERE, PETE -- I'M NOT CRACKIN' ON YOUR STYLE, BUT IT IS KINDA *COZY*.

I STILL CAN'T WORK OUT WHY YOU WANTED TO MOVE OUT OF OUR APARTMENT IN THE *FIRST* PLACE, AMIGO. WE WERE THE ENVY OF EVERY OTHER LOSER ON THE BLOCK.

THIS DIDN'T HAVE SOMETHING TO DO WITH MARY JANE LEAVING, DID IT? I MEAN, 'CAUSE IF SO, I CAN ALWAYS GO TRACK HER BUTT DOWN AN' DRAG HER BACK HERE.

DON'T TAKE IT PERSONALLY, RANDY. I JUST NEEDED MY *SPACE,* Y'KNOW?

MM. IMAGINE THE IRONY OF FINDING IT IN *THIS* SARDINE CAN. SERIOUSLY, DUDE... WHY THE HECK WOULD YOU EVER WANNA --

HI, PETER! **YOO HOO!**

WELL... THAT'S *THAT* LITTLE MYSTERY SOLVED.

HI, CARYN. HOW'S THE, UH... WEATHER?

OH, GOD... IT'S SO *HUMID* IN THE CITY RIGHT NOW. I *HATE* IT WHEN IT GETS LIKE THIS.

OUR AIR-CONDITIONING BROKE LAST WEEK AN' THE LANDLORD STILL HASN'T BEEN ROUND TO *FIX* IT. I HAVE TO JUST LIE AROUND NAKED UNDER THE FANS ALL THE TIME.

IT MAKES BARKER NERVOUS -- HE'S A REAL *PRUDE* ABOUT STUFF LIKE THAT.

YEAH, THAT MUST BE REAL AWKWARD FOR HIM. CONSIDERING HE'S A *DOG*, AN' ALL.

I'LL, UH... I'LL CATCH YOU LATER, OKAY?

SOUNDS GOOD TO ME. DON'T BE A *STRANGER*, HANDSOME.

C'MON, BARKER...

DUDE, SHE TOTALLY DIGS YOU. THAT WAS *SHAMELESS!*

YEAH, BUT I'M NOT SO SURE ABOUT THAT NEUROTIC DOG OF HERS. THAT MUTT GIVES ME THE *WILLIES.*

Three Hundred

Paul Jenkins Writer Mark Buckingham Pencils Wayne Faucher Inks
Jung Choi Colors Richard Starkings & Comicraft's Oscar Gongora Letters
John Miesegaes Ass't Ed Axel Alonso Editor Joe Quesada Editor In Chief

...→UNNH←...
TWO HUNDRED
AND NINETY-
NINE...

...AU-UHH...
THREE
HUNDRED!

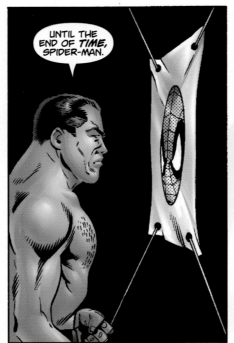

UNTIL THE END OF *TIME,* SPIDER-MAN.

UNTIL THE END OF TIME, AND THE DAY AFTER *THAT.* A HATRED THAT RUNS SO DEEP --

-- RUNS FOREVER.

RRRIIIPP

HI, THIS IS PETER. I'M STILL SETTLING INTO MY NEW DIGS, SO I'M EITHER WORKING, OUT FORAGING FOR FOOD, OR TRAPPED UNDER DEBRIS. LEAVE A MESSAGE AND I'LL GET BACK TO YOU WHEN THE DUST CLEARS.

BEEEEEP

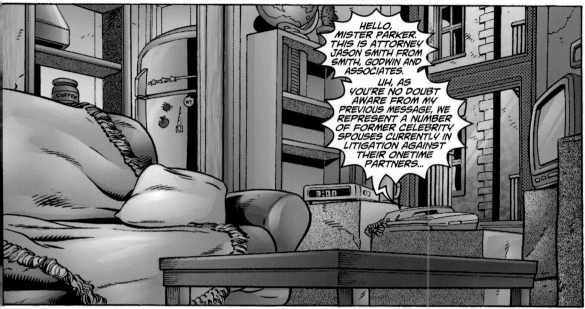

HELLO, MISTER PARKER. THIS IS ATTORNEY JASON SMITH FROM SMITH, GODWIN AND ASSOCIATES.

UH, AS YOU'RE NO DOUBT AWARE FROM MY PREVIOUS MESSAGE, WE REPRESENT A NUMBER OF FORMER CELEBRITY SPOUSES CURRENTLY IN LITIGATION AGAINST THEIR ONETIME PARTNERS...

... AND SINCE SO MANY OF OUR CLIENTS HAVE BEEN AWARDED SUBSTANTIAL SETTLEMENTS AS A RESULT OF OUR REPRESENTATION, WE WERE HOPING...

...TO HEAR FROM YOU AT YOUR EARLIEST CONVENIENCE...

RRR...

SNFF
SNFF

IT'S SUNDAY, AND THE VULTURES ARE CIRCLING OVER THE SKELETAL REMAINS OF MY FORMER LIFE.

JUST MY LUCK: YOU FIGURE EARTH PROBABLY HAS 0.0001 PERCENT OF THE GALAXY'S POPULATION, BUT WE'VE STILL GOT 95 PERCENT OF THE LAWYERS.

HALF OF WHOM HAVE CALLED ME IN THE LAST WEEK.

BUT IT'S FUNNY... THERE ARE DAYS WHEN THAT KIND OF THING CAN HAVE YOU LYING FACE DOWN ON THE SOFA, UNABLE TO DREDGE UP THE ENERGY TO EVEN CHANGE CHANNELS ON THE TV.

TODAY, THOUGH, I CAN ACTUALLY FEEL THE SUN SHINING... EVEN ON ME. IT'S AMAZING HOW YOU CAN FEEL WEIGHED DOWN AND LIBERATED AT THE SAME TIME.

RANDY'S BEEN SUCH A GOOD GUY ABOUT ME MOVING OUT ON SUCH SHORT NOTICE. I PROBABLY OWE HIM A TON OF RENT MONEY AND HE'S NEVER ONCE ASKED ME FOR IT.

IN THE MEANTIME, THE NEW PLACE SUITS ME JUST FINE... IT'S GOING TO GIVE ME A CHANCE TO DETERMINE MY FUTURE, TO RUMINATE ON LIFE'S LITTLE QUIRKS.

IT'S IDEALLY SITUATED, TOO -- THE PERFECT PLACE FOR AN UNDERAPPRECIATED WEBSLINGER TO HIDE IN PLAIN SIGHT. IT'S SMALL AND QUIET AND THE ROOF'S EASY TO ACCESS. NOBODY'S EVER GOING TO KNOW THAT I'M COMING UP HERE...

... NOT UNLESS YOU COUNT MY CANINE FRIEND ACROSS THE WAY.

THE MIGHTY BARKER: I SWEAR, THIS HAS *GOT* TO BE THE MOST RIDICULOUS CREATURE THIS SIDE OF NEW JERSEY.

I CAN'T TELL IF HE ADORES ME OR *HATES* ME. IF ONLY HE COULD TALK, I WONDER WHAT HE'D SAY?

I WON'T TELL IF *YOU* DON'T, PAL.

MAYBE IT'S MY IMAGINATION. IT'S JUST... IT'S AS IF HE HAS SOME KIND OF SECRET DOGGY AGENDA THAT INVOLVES *ME* SOMEHOW. IT'S LIKE WE'RE SETTING OFF EACH OTHER'S MENTAL ALARMS.

POP
WH/RR
BZZZZ

AND AS WEIRD AS THIS SOUNDS, I CAN'T SHAKE THE FEELING HE'S BUILDING SOMETHING IN THERE...

HEY THERE, YOU IN THE *MASK!* YOU MIND TELLING ME WHERE YOU'RE GOING WITH ALL THAT STUFF? YOU HAVE AN *APPOINTMENT* HERE TODAY?

SIR, I HAVE TO CAUTION YOU-- SECURITY'S PRETTY TIGHT AROUND HERE RIGHT NOW. SOMEONE COMES BY DRESSED FOR MARDI GRAS, I GOTTA ASK MYSELF, "WHY?"

NOW, I ASKED YOU POLITELY THE FIRST TIME. STATE YOUR NAME AND *BUSINESS*, PLEASE--

CAUTION DRY ICE

HANDLE WITH CARE

NO.

AAH!

SMASH

HEY, WHAT THE--?

YOU! STOP RIGHT THERE!

OOPS!

DODGERS

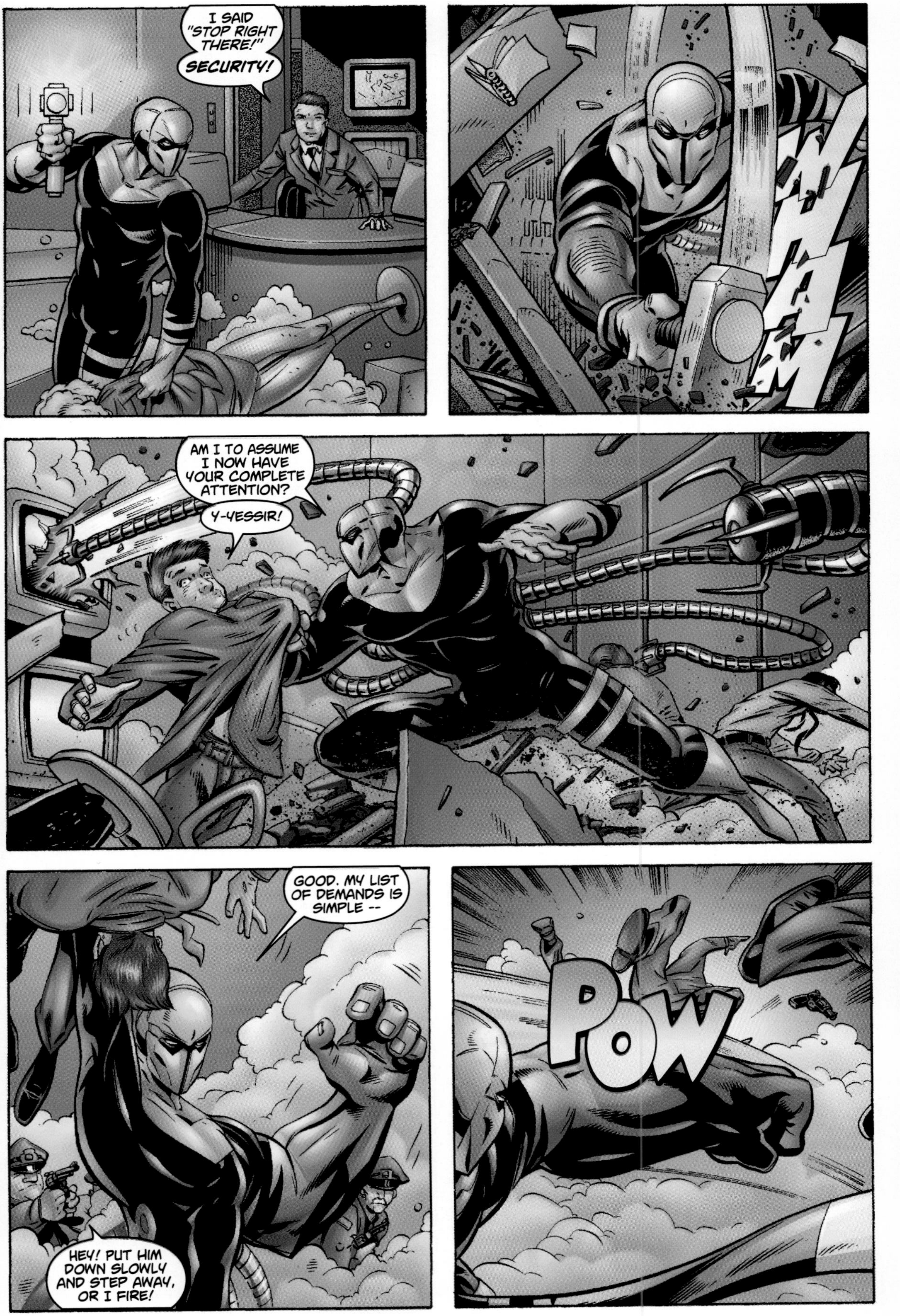
I SAID "STOP RIGHT THERE!" SECURITY!
WHAM
AM I TO ASSUME I NOW HAVE YOUR COMPLETE ATTENTION?
Y-YESSIR!
GOOD. MY LIST OF DEMANDS IS SIMPLE --
HEY! PUT HIM DOWN SLOWLY AND STEP AWAY, OR I FIRE!
POW

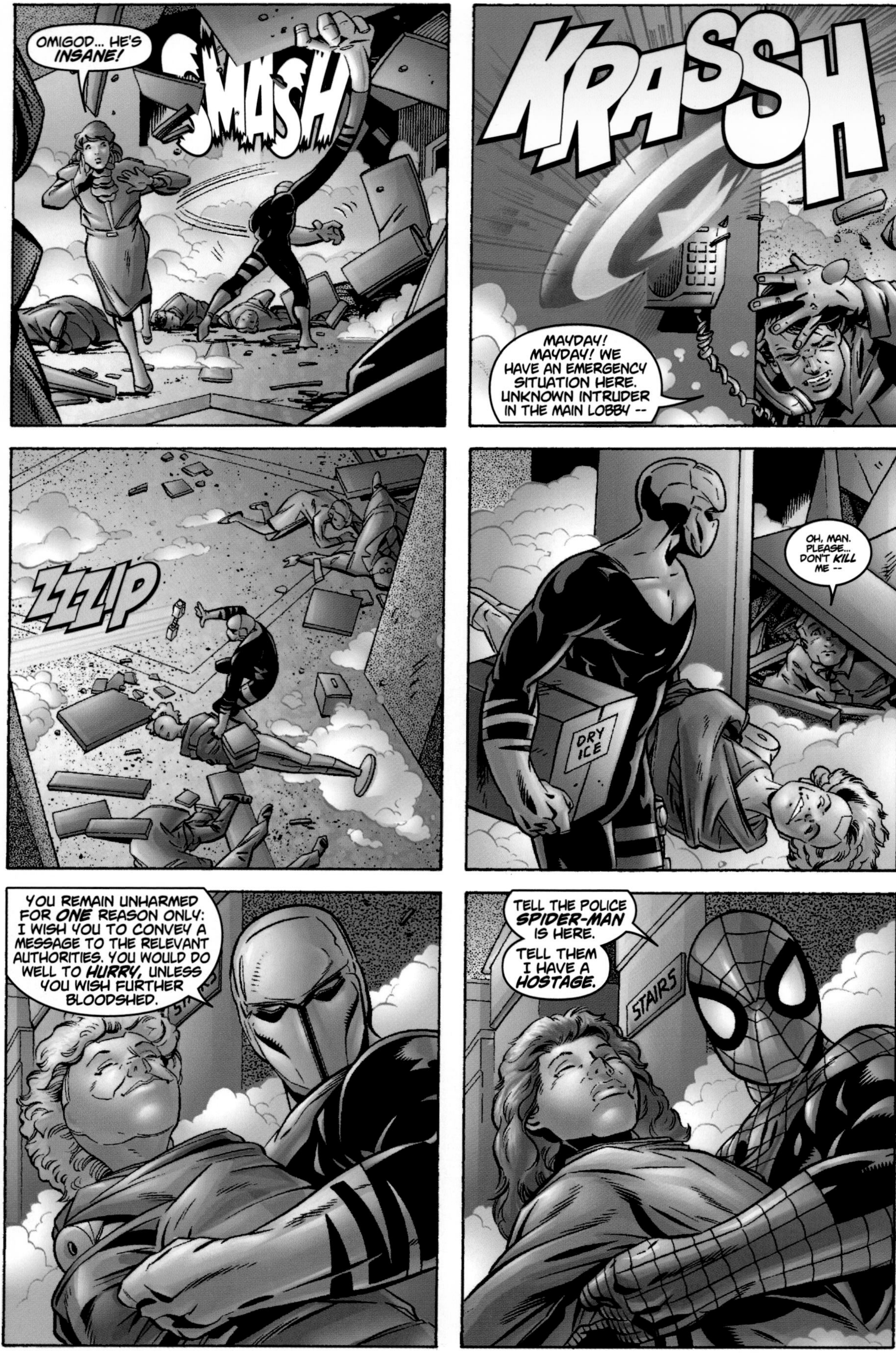
OMIGOD... HE'S INSANE!
SMASH
KRASSH
MAYDAY! MAYDAY! WE HAVE AN EMERGENCY SITUATION HERE. UNKNOWN INTRUDER IN THE MAIN LOBBY --
ZZZIP
OH, MAN. PLEASE... DON'T KILL ME --
DRY ICE
YOU REMAIN UNHARMED FOR ONE REASON ONLY: I WISH YOU TO CONVEY A MESSAGE TO THE RELEVANT AUTHORITIES. YOU WOULD DO WELL TO HURRY, UNLESS YOU WISH FURTHER BLOODSHED.
TELL THE POLICE SPIDER-MAN IS HERE.
TELL THEM I HAVE A HOSTAGE.
STAIRS

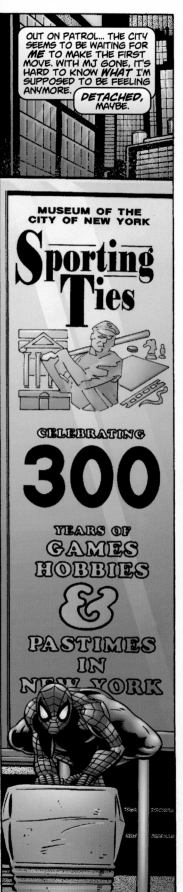

OUT ON PATROL... THE CITY SEEMS TO BE WAITING FOR *ME* TO MAKE THE FIRST MOVE. WITH MJ GONE, IT'S HARD TO KNOW *WHAT* I'M SUPPOSED TO BE FEELING ANYMORE. *DETACHED*, MAYBE.

MUSEUM OF THE CITY OF NEW YORK

Sporting Ties

CELEBRATING

300

YEARS OF GAMES HOBBIES & PASTIMES IN NEW YORK

I GUESS MY SENSE OF UNEASE IS NATURAL: I LOSE MY WIFE, ONLY TO FIND HER AGAIN. ONLY TO SEE HER *GO* AGAIN. MAYBE IT'S ALL THE UNCERTAINTY THAT'S MAKING MY NERVE ENDINGS JANGLE.

BUT SOMETHING'S COMING DOWN THE PIKE -- I CAN *FEEL* IT. IT'S A TWELVE-TON TRUCK OF COMPLICATIONS, AND ITS BRAKES DON'T WORK.

ME, I'M JUST A LITTLE OLD SPIDER CROSSING THE ROAD.

AH, WELL... ALL THINGS BEING EQUAL, IT'S A NICE NIGHT TO BE OUT ON THE TOWN. I WONDER WHY IT'S SO *QUIET*..?

... CONTINUING OUR COUNTDOWN OF THE HUNDRED WORST SONGS OF ALL TIME WITH NUMBER FIFTY-SEVEN: *WALKING TO DESTRUCTION* BY *GRAVE GOODS*... SKKRT...

... AN' SO I'M TELLIN' HER WE NEED TO SPICE UP OUR *LOVE* LIFE, AN' SHE COMES HOME WITH A FEATHER DUSTER AN' A GALLON OF COD LIVER OIL. SHE *KNOWS* I'M ALLERGIC TO FEATHERS... SKKRT...

... I MEAN, TWENTY MILLION A YEAR, AND HE TURNS IT *DOWN?* WHATTA MAROON...

... LIFE IN THE FAST LA-ANE... SKKRT...

... A TENSE HOSTAGE SITUATION HIGH ABOVE THE CITY ON THE ROOF OF THE *EDGAR TOWER.* DETAILS ARE SKETCHY AT PRESENT, BUT ONE INTERCEPTED POLICE REPORT SUGGESTS THE PERPETRATOR IS NONE OTHER THAN *SPIDER-MAN* --

WELL, THAT ANSWERS *THAT* QUESTION.

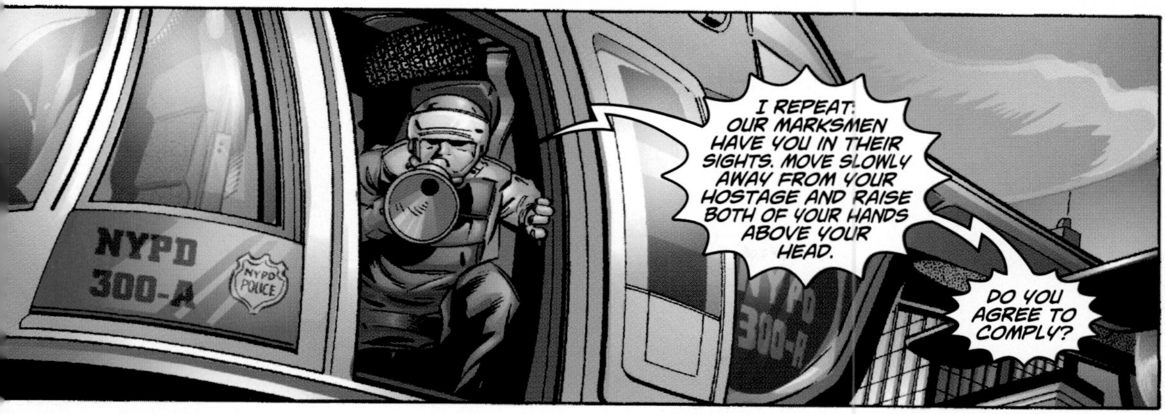
NYPD
300-A
NYPD POLICE
I REPEAT: OUR MARKSMEN HAVE YOU IN THEIR SIGHTS. MOVE SLOWLY AWAY FROM YOUR HOSTAGE AND RAISE BOTH OF YOUR HANDS ABOVE YOUR HEAD.
DO YOU AGREE TO COMPLY?

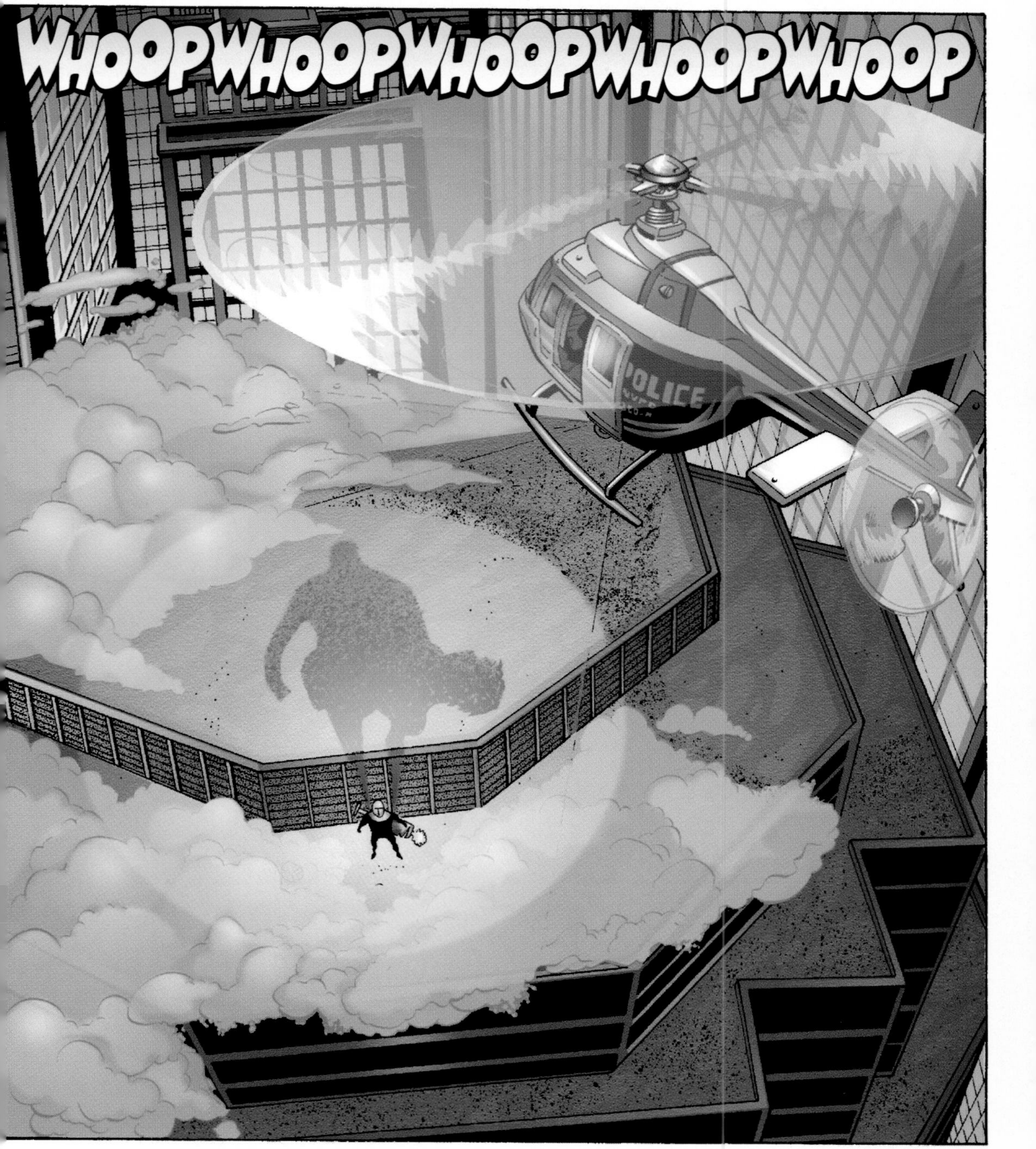
WHOOPWHOOPWHOOPWHOOPWHOOP
POLICE

WHAT'S HE DOING?

I DUNNO, SARGE -- HE HASN'T SAID A WORD SINCE WE GOT HERE. NO ONE CAN GET THROUGH TO HIM.

I THOUGHT YOU SAID IT WAS SPIDER-MAN. THAT DON'T LOOK LIKE SPIDER-MAN TO ME.

I-IT WAS. I MEAN, WE **THOUGHT** IT WAS WHEN WE **GOT** HERE, BUT IT'S LIKE HE **CHANGED**, OR SOMETHIN'. DON'T ASK ME HOW.

I WON'T. JUST MAKE SURE YOU GET THE RIGHT DESCRIPTION OUT TO THE PRESS NEXT TIME --

-- LOOK **THERE!**

I KNEW YOU WOULD COME SCURRYING, SPIDER-MAN. HEROIC AS CLOCKWORK.

YOU'LL HAVE TO REFRESH MY MEMORY, PAL: I THOUGHT I KNEW ALL THE POORLY-DRESSED SOCIOPATHS IN TOWN.

YOU *NEW* TO OUR JAIL SYSTEM, OR JUST VISITING?

I MAKE YOU THIS PROMISE HERE AND NOW: YOU'RE NOT GOING TO DEFEAT ME. NOT EVER.

BEFORE THIS DAY IS OVER, YOU'LL REGRET THAT YOU EVER LAID EYES ON ME, AND EVEN MORE SO THAT YOU EVER CHOSE TO WEAR THAT COSTUME OF YOURS. YOUR LIFE AS YOU KNEW IT ENDS *NOW.*

WELL, DON'T I FEEL SPECIAL. YOU GOT A *NAME* TO GO WITH THAT EGO? I MEAN, IT'S ALWAYS NICE TO KNOW WHOSE *FACE* YOU'RE ABOUT TO BEAT INTO AN UNRECOGNIZABLE PULP --

WHACK

I DON'T FIND YOU *AMUSING,* SPIDER-MAN.

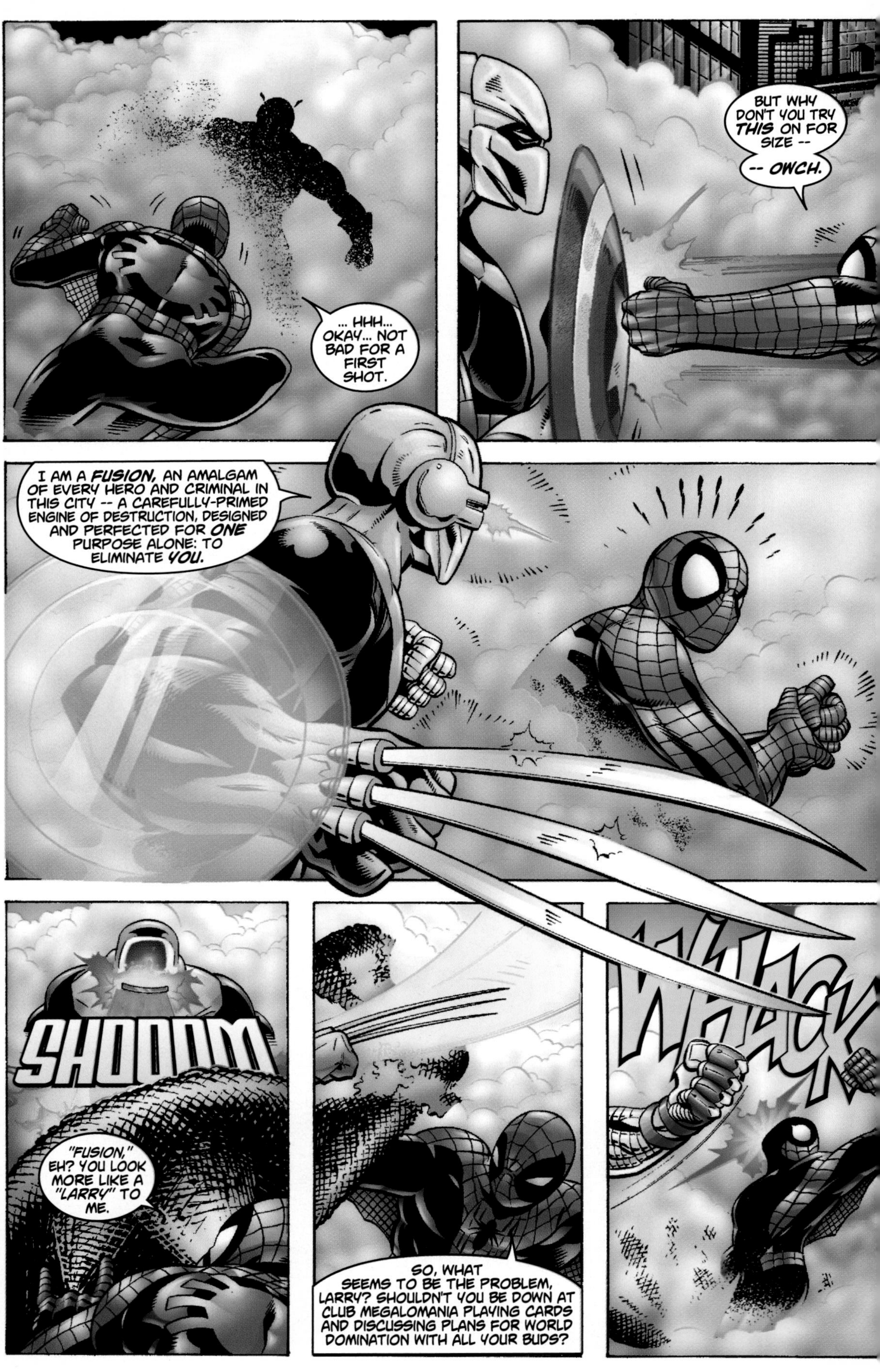
... HHH... OKAY... NOT BAD FOR A FIRST SHOT.
BUT WHY DON'T YOU TRY THIS ON FOR SIZE --
-- OWCH.
I AM A FUSION, AN AMALGAM OF EVERY HERO AND CRIMINAL IN THIS CITY -- A CAREFULLY-PRIMED ENGINE OF DESTRUCTION, DESIGNED AND PERFECTED FOR ONE PURPOSE ALONE: TO ELIMINATE YOU.
SHOOOM
"FUSION," EH? YOU LOOK MORE LIKE A "LARRY" TO ME.
SO, WHAT SEEMS TO BE THE PROBLEM, LARRY? SHOULDN'T YOU BE DOWN AT CLUB MEGALOMANIA PLAYING CARDS AND DISCUSSING PLANS FOR WORLD DOMINATION WITH ALL YOUR BUDS?
WHACK

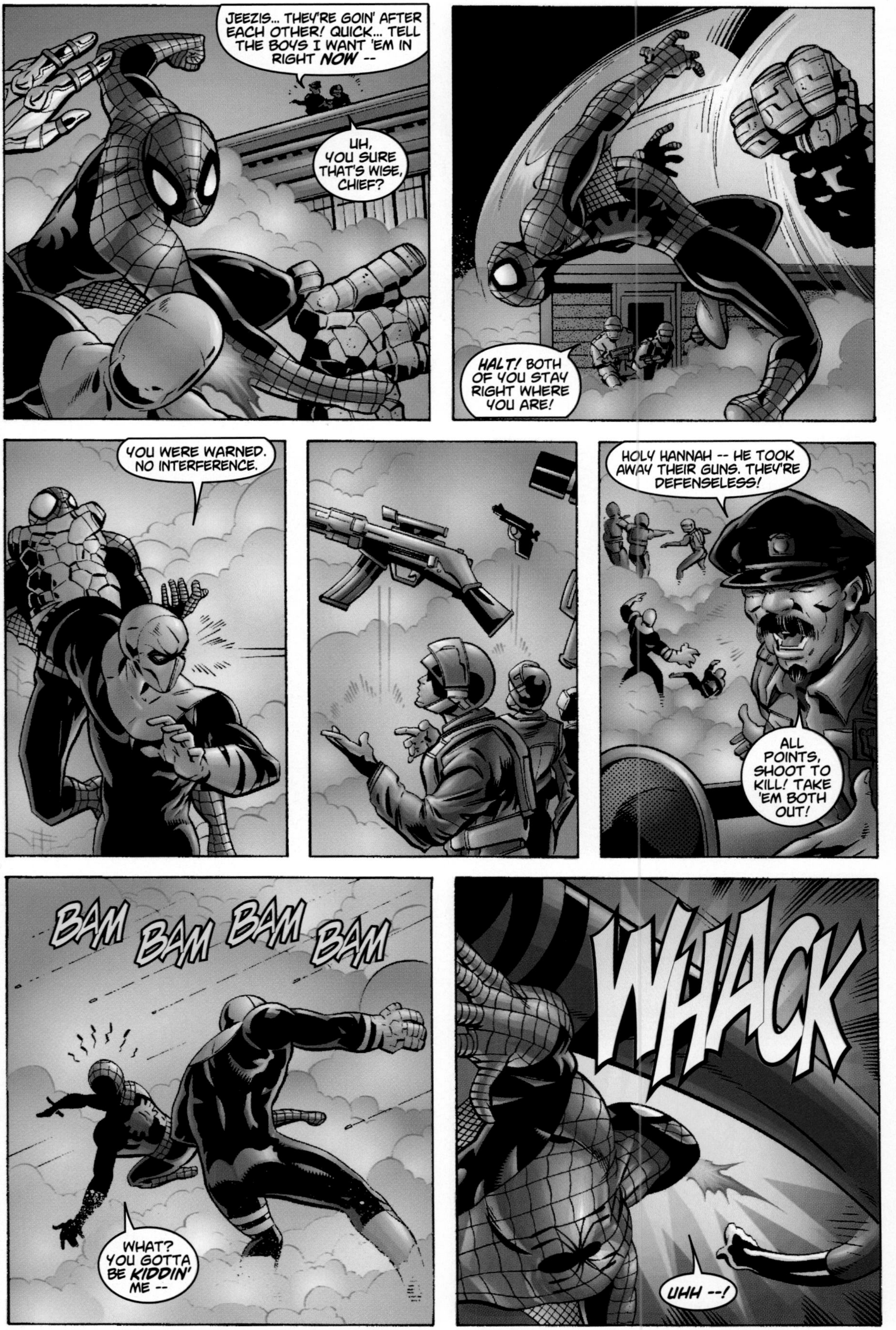

JEEZIS... THEY'RE GOIN' AFTER EACH OTHER! QUICK... TELL THE BOYS I WANT 'EM IN RIGHT NOW --
UH, YOU SURE THAT'S WISE, CHIEF?
HALT! BOTH OF YOU STAY RIGHT WHERE YOU ARE!
YOU WERE WARNED. NO INTERFERENCE.
HOLY HANNAH -- HE TOOK AWAY THEIR GUNS. THEY'RE DEFENSELESS!
ALL POINTS, SHOOT TO KILL! TAKE 'EM BOTH OUT!
BAM BAM BAM BAM
WHAT? YOU GOTTA BE KIDDIN' ME --
WHACK
UHH --!

DIE!

THOOM

AA-AH!

EXPLODE.

OMIGOD --?

BOOOM

YOU DIDN'T HAVE TO DO THAT. I'VE SEEN ENOUGH TO KNOW YOU WEREN'T GOING TO BE AFFECTED BY THEIR GUNS.

WHY COULDN'T YOU JUST LET THEM LIVE?

BECAUSE OF *YOU.*

THERE WAS ONCE A VERY BEAUTIFUL LITTLE BOY, WITH CLOSE BLOND CURLS. A *SERIOUS* CHILD, WHO NONETHELESS ALWAYS HAD A SMILE FOR HIS FATHER.

SCHOOL WAS *HARD* FOR A CHILD SO PAINFULLY SHY -- HIS TEACHERS THOUGHT HIM SLOW-WITTED, AND SOME OF THE OTHER CHILDREN PICKED ON HIM.

SO HE ESCAPED IN DAYDREAMS. MOST OF ALL, HE ADORED SPIDER-MAN.

THE BOY THOUGHT HE MIGHT *EMULATE* HIS HERO. TO BE SPIDER-MAN WAS INFINITELY PREFERABLE, HE THOUGHT, TO FACING HIS PEERS IN THE PLAYGROUND...

... AND SO HE WENT TO THE TOP OF AN OLD WAREHOUSE, ARMED WITH A LENGTH OF ROPE AND HIS IMAGINATION. HE JUMPED, EXPECTING TO SWING.

SO MUCH FOR *EXPECTATIONS*.

I'M NOT GOING TO KILL YOU, SPIDER-MAN. NOT *TODAY*. I'M GOING TO MAKE YOU *PAY* FIRST. THESE PEOPLE WHO DIED... I WANT YOU TO UNDERSTAND WHOSE *FAULT* IT WAS. I WANT YOU TO LIVE WITH THAT.

PEOPLE WHO DIED? WHAT DO YOU MEAN?

THESE PEOPLE --

WAIT -- **NO!**

BUT IT'S TOO LATE. EVENTS HAVE BEEN SET IN SLOW-MOTION. THERE'S NOTHING I CAN DO TO STOP THEM.

I'M A SPIDER, SCUTTLING ACROSS THE MIDDLE OF A BUSY ROAD. I CAN SEE HEADLIGHTS COMING MY WAY.

THAT SENSE OF UNEASE IS REPLACED BY A FEELING OF **DREAD**.

I LOOK UP, JUST AS A TWELVE-TON TRUCKLOAD OF COMPLICATIONS COMES CRASHING DOWN FROM ABOVE.

A FINAL THOUGHT FLASHES ACROSS MY MIND: HAVEN'T I BEEN HERE **BEFORE?**

AND THAT'S WHEN IT **HITS** ME.

0:00

TIK

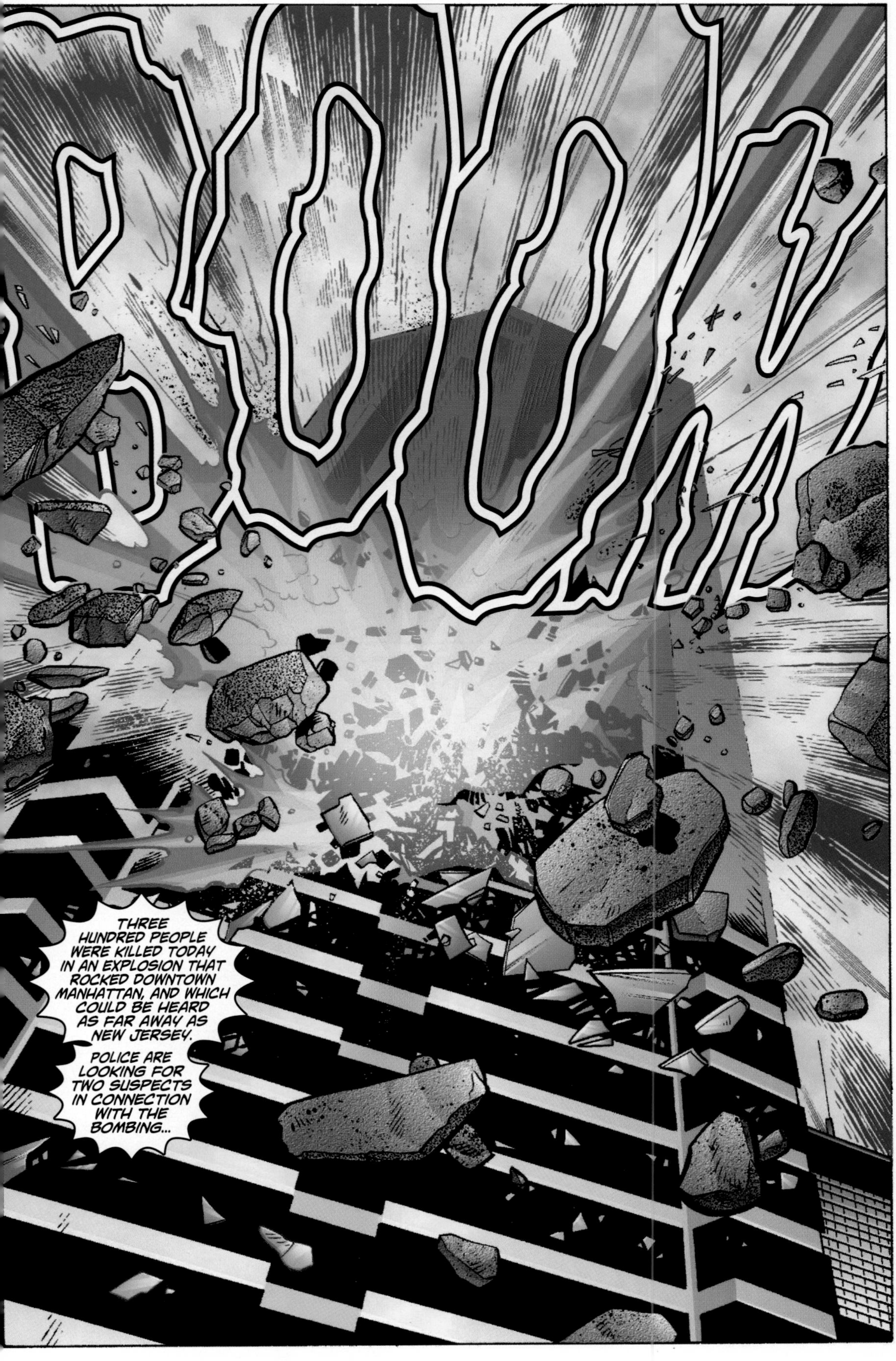
THREE HUNDRED PEOPLE WERE KILLED TODAY IN AN EXPLOSION THAT ROCKED DOWNTOWN MANHATTAN, AND WHICH COULD BE HEARD AS FAR AWAY AS NEW JERSEY.
POLICE ARE LOOKING FOR TWO SUSPECTS IN CONNECTION WITH THE BOMBING...

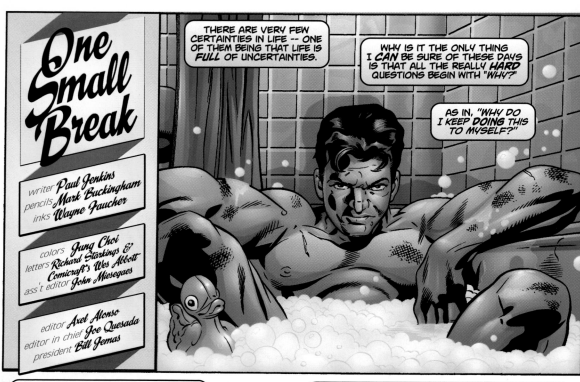

One Small Break

writer *Paul Jenkins*
pencils *Mark Buckingham*
inks *Wayne Faucher*

colors *Jung Choi*
letters *Richard Starkings &*
Comicraft's Wes Abbott
ass't editor *John Miesegaes*

editor *Axel Alonso*
editor in chief *Joe Quesada*
president *Bill Jemas*

THERE ARE VERY FEW CERTAINTIES IN LIFE -- ONE OF THEM BEING THAT LIFE IS *FULL* OF UNCERTAINTIES.

WHY IS IT THE ONLY THING I *CAN* BE SURE OF THESE DAYS IS THAT ALL THE REALLY *HARD* QUESTIONS BEGIN WITH "WHY?"

AS IN, "WHY DO I KEEP *DOING* THIS TO MYSELF?"

TAKE THIS GUY, FUSION, FOR EXAMPLE. JUST ANOTHER NUTZOID WHO HAPPENS TO WALTZ IN ARMED WITH EVERY SUPER-POWER EVER INVENTED, AND PROCEEDS TO CLEAN MY CLOCK ON NATIONAL TELEVISION, RIGHT?

WRONG. THE GUY WAS BIGGER, STRONGER, FASTER AND *BETTER* THAN ME...AND WORST OF ALL, HE DIDN'T SO MUCH AS REGISTER A *BLIP* ON MY SPIDER-SENSE.

NEITHER DID THE *BOMB* HE DROPPED ON THE BUILDING BELOW US -- NOT UNTIL IT WAS TOO LATE. THREE HUNDRED PEOPLE DIED BECAUSE OF FUSION'S HATRED FOR ME. AND I NEVER EVEN SAW IT *COMING*.

ALL OF WHICH MAKES ME ASK "WHY?" WHY DO I PUT ON THE MASK -- DAY IN AND DAY OUT -- ONLY TO SUFFER THE ABUSE OF AN INDIFFERENT PUBLIC AND THE OCCASIONAL ROUND OF POLICE GUNFIRE?

SOMETIMES, I JUST WANT TO SHOUT FROM THE ROOFTOPS, "HEY! MY NAME IS PETER PARKER AND I'M TRYING MY *BEST* UP HERE."

IT'S TIMES LIKE THESE I JUST WISH I COULD COME *CLEAN*.

I DON'T KNOW... MAYBE THIS WHOLE HERO THING IS JUST IN MY *NATURE*. IT'S AS IF I'M ADDICTED TO MARTYRDOM, OR SOMETHING.

BUT I CAN'T HELP WONDERING HOW MANY OTHER PEOPLE WOULD DO WHAT I DO? WHO'D PERFORM A NOBLE, SELFLESS ACT -- JUST ONCE, WITHOUT TAKING CREDIT FOR IT?

WHAT DOES IT SAY ABOUT ME THAT I DO IT EVERY *DAY*?

HI, THIS IS PETER. I'M STILL SETTLING INTO MY NEW DIGS, SO I'M EITHER WORKING, OUT FORAGING FOR FOOD, OR TRAPPED UNDER DEBRIS. LEAVE A MESSAGE AND I'LL GET BACK TO YOU WHEN THE DUST CLEARS.

BEEEEP

HI, PETER! IT'S CARYN EARLE FROM ACROSS THE WAY. Y'KNOW... YOUR NEW NEIGHBOR?

LISTEN, I WAS WONDERING IF YOU COULD DO ME A FAVOR? I'M GOING OUT OF TOWN AND I WON'T BE BACK FOR A COUPLE OF DAYS. I WAS HOPING YOU COULD FEED BARKER FOR ME WHILE I'M GONE?

HE'S SUCH A GOOD BOY -- I KNOW HE WON'T BE ANY TROUBLE. HE REALLY SEEMS TO LIKE YOU A LOT, Y'KNOW.

PLEASE? IT'D BE SUCH A HELP. I'LL TALK TO YOU. BYE!

NOT IF YOU PAID ME A MILLION BUCKS, BLONDIE.

NOPE. FOR ONE AFTERNOON, THE OLD PARKER CONSCIENCE IS ON VACATION, TRANSFERRING ITS OFFICIAL DUTIES OVER TO THE PARKER DIGESTIVE SYSTEM...

MM... CHOICES, CHOICES. "PORK WITH TINKLING BELLS." DO I DARE...?

OH, GREAT. NICE HANDS, RIPKEN --

DONK

KNOCK KNOCK

HI, PETER...I SAW YOU WERE IN, SO I CAME OVER! IT'S CARYN! FROM ACROSS THE WAY!

UH, YEAH... I KNOW. CAN YOU GIVE ME A SECOND, CARYN?

I CAN'T HEAR YOU -- WHAT'D YOU SAY?

I SAID, "DON'T COME IN!"

OH, OKAY.

YOU DID SAY "COME IN," RIGHT?

ERM. NOT RIGHT AT THE MOMENT, NO. I WASN'T, UH... *EXPECTING* ANYONE.

I MEAN, Y'KNOW... I'M HARDLY DRESSED FOR IT.

YOU LOOK FINE FROM WHERE I'M STANDING. DON'T WORRY 'BOUT ME -- I'M NOT OFFENDED BY NUDITY.

GOOD FOR YOU. LISTEN, CARYN --

SAY, YOU GOT ANY SODA IN THE FRIDGE? I'M PARCHED.

YOU LOOK A LOT FITTER CLOSE UP, PETER. WHERE D'YOU WORK OUT?

OH, UH... ALL *OVER*, REALLY.

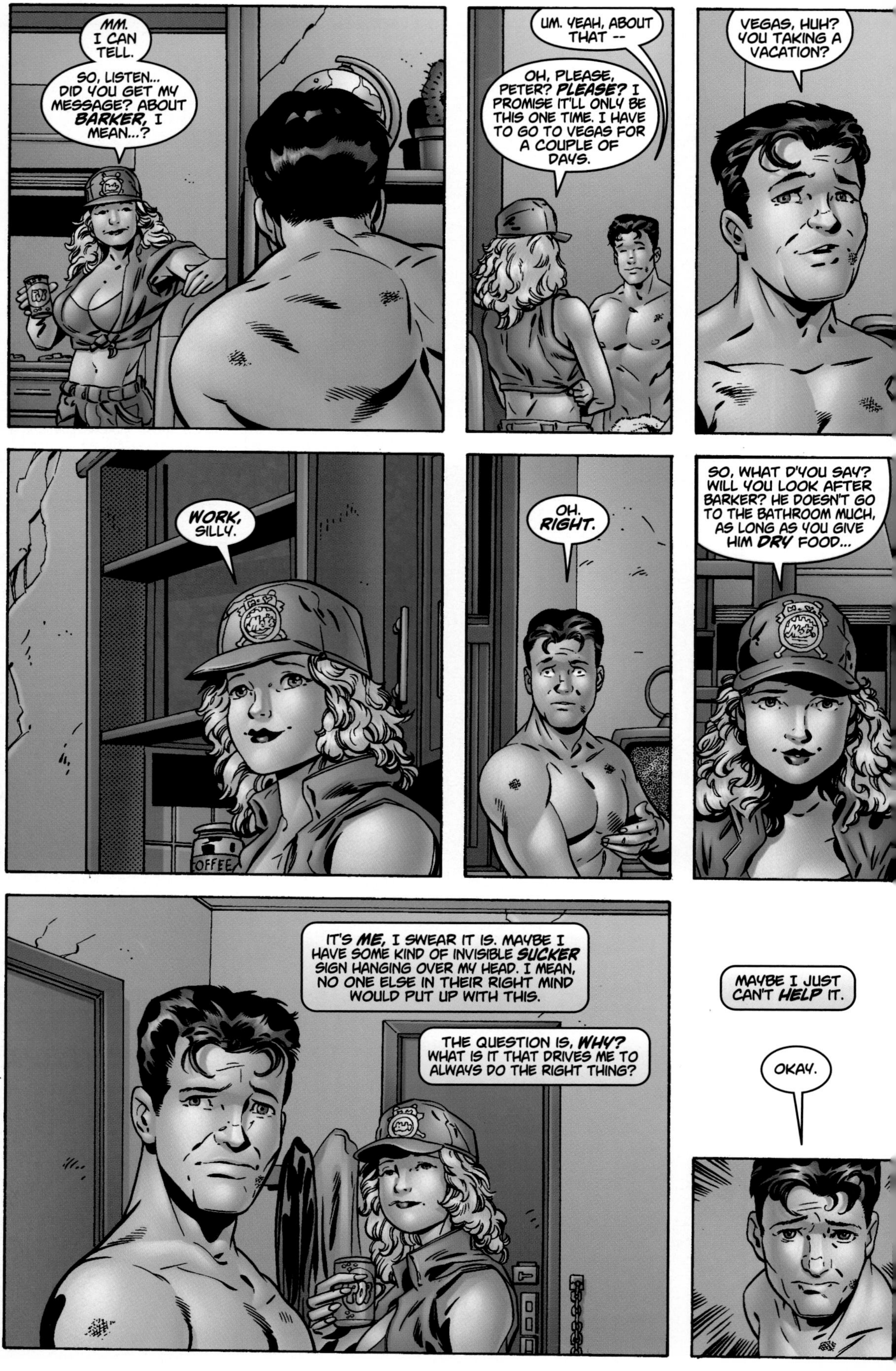
MM. I CAN TELL.
SO, LISTEN... DID YOU GET MY MESSAGE? ABOUT BARKER, I MEAN...?
UM. YEAH, ABOUT THAT --
OH, PLEASE, PETER? PLEASE? I PROMISE IT'LL ONLY BE THIS ONE TIME. I HAVE TO GO TO VEGAS FOR A COUPLE OF DAYS.
VEGAS, HUH? YOU TAKING A VACATION?
WORK, SILLY.
OH. RIGHT.
SO, WHAT D'YOU SAY? WILL YOU LOOK AFTER BARKER? HE DOESN'T GO TO THE BATHROOM MUCH, AS LONG AS YOU GIVE HIM DRY FOOD...
COFFEE
IT'S ME, I SWEAR IT IS. MAYBE I HAVE SOME KIND OF INVISIBLE SUCKER SIGN HANGING OVER MY HEAD. I MEAN, NO ONE ELSE IN THEIR RIGHT MIND WOULD PUT UP WITH THIS.
THE QUESTION IS, WHY? WHAT IS IT THAT DRIVES ME TO ALWAYS DO THE RIGHT THING?
MAYBE I JUST CAN'T HELP IT.
OKAY.

PEOPLE OF NEW YORK: MY NAME IS FUSION.

I HEREBY CLAIM RESPONSIBILITY FOR THE RECENT BOMBING OF THE EDGAR TOWER WHICH HAS TAKEN THE LIVES OF THREE HUNDRED OF YOUR FELLOW CITIZENS.

I WANT YOU ALL TO ASK YOURSELF ONE SIMPLE QUESTION TODAY: WHY? WHY WOULD A MAN RAIN SUCH DEATH AND DESTRUCTION UPON OUR FAIR CITY WHEN WE HAVE DONE NO WRONG?

MY RESPONSE IS EQUALLY SIMPLE: THIS WAS NOT THE WORK OF JUST ONE MAN. FOR AS SURELY AS I PREPARED THE DEVICE, IT CAN BE SAID THAT THE COSTUMED "HERO," SPIDER-MAN, SUPPLIED THE IMPETUS FOR ITS CONSTRUCTION.

A SOMEWHAT **BIZARRE** STATEMENT, THEN, FROM THIS ALLEGED PERPETRATOR OF DOMESTIC TERRORISM -- THE SUPER-VILLAIN KNOWN TO US ONLY AS FUSION.

LIVE HERE AT THE NINETEENTH PRECINCT, I HAVE WITH ME NOTED CRIMINOLOGIST, DR. ANDREW McCULLOUGH...

YES, VERY BIZARRE INDEED...GIVEN THAT WITNESSES CLEARLY OBSERVED SPIDER-MAN MAKING A CONCERTED EFFORT TO STOP THE BOMBING, RISKING HIS OWN LIFE IN THE PROCESS.

FROM FUSION'S STATEMENTS, WE CAN INFER THAT HE BLAMES SPIDER-MAN FOR SOME PREVIOUS TRANSGRESSION, IMAGINED OR OTHERWISE.

THIS BRINGS UP AN INTERESTING QUESTION, ONE THAT HAS BEEN ASKED MANY TIMES BEFORE: HAD THERE BEEN NO SPIDER-MAN, WOULD THERE HAVE BEEN NO BOMBING ALSO?

I WOULD SAY OPINIONS ARE VARIED... EVEN IF SPIDER-MAN IS MERELY A TARGET OF THIS MAN'S FIXATION, HIS VERY PRESENCE IN THE CITY HAS GIVEN A LOT OF PEOPLE CAUSE FOR CONCERN --

ANY WAY WE CAN GET SOME MILEAGE OUT OF THIS, ROBBIE? CAN WE USE THIS ANGLE TO GO AFTER SPIDER-MAN?

NOT LIKELY, CHIEF. LOOKS LIKE THE NETWORKS HAVE IT PRETTY WELL COVERED.

RUN IT ON PAGE SEVEN, THEN.

AND SO, ONE WOULD EXPECT SOME VERY DIFFICULT QUESTIONS ARE GOING TO BE RAISED ABOUT THE WALL-CRAWLING VIGILANTE, WHO SEEMS TO HAVE BECOME A FIXTURE IN THE CITY OVER THE LAST FEW YEARS.

REPORTING LIVE FROM THE NINETEENTH PRECINCT, THIS IS BRENT WILLIFORD. NOW, BACK TO THE STUDIO...

THANKS, BRENT... AND IN A FURTHER DEVELOPMENT, POLICE HAVE RELEASED A SECOND PORTION OF THE VIDEOTAPE WHICH APPEARS TO BE AIMED DIRECTLY AT SPIDER-MAN HIMSELF...

...ALTHOUGH WHETHER OR NOT THE MAN BEHIND THE MASK IS WATCHING THIS BROADCAST, ONLY TIME WILL TELL.

COFFEE

TO THE INSECT KNOWN AS SPIDER-MAN, I HEREBY ISSUE A CHALLENGE: I HAVE DEFEATED YOU IN BATTLE ONCE. WILL YOU FACE ME A SECOND TIME?

THE FATE OF THOUSANDS IS IN YOUR HANDS. IF YOU IGNORE THIS... INVITATION, OTHERS WILL MOST ASSUREDLY DIE. THERE IS NOTHING THAT CAN BE DONE TO STOP ME.

AT THIS MOMENT, A HUNDRED DEVICES SIMILAR TO THE ONE THAT DESTROYED THE EDGAR BUILDING ARE SPREAD ACROSS THE CITY AT RANDOM, READY TO BE DETONATED UNLESS YOU FIND THE COURAGE TO SACRIFICE YOURSELF TO ME.

YOU HAVEN'T THE CAPACITY TO STAND AGAINST ME, SPIDER-MAN. AND YET STAND AGAINST ME YOU MUST. ONLY YOU HAVE THE REQUISITE PIECES OF THE PUZZLE TO UNDERSTAND WHAT TO DO NEXT.

YOU WILL KNOW WHERE TO GO, IF YOU CONSIDER THE INFORMATION I SUPPLIED TO YOU DURING OUR LAST ENCOUNTER.

MEET ME --

CLICK

-- WHERE THE ANGELS FALL.

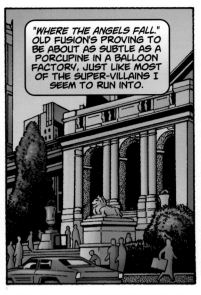

"WHERE THE ANGELS FALL." OLD FUSION'S PROVING TO BE ABOUT AS SUBTLE AS A PORCUPINE IN A BALLOON FACTORY, JUST LIKE MOST OF THE SUPER-VILLAINS I SEEM TO RUN INTO.

JUDGING BY THE INFORMATION HE SLIPPED ME AT THE EDGAR TOWER, IT'S CLEAR FUSION BLAMES ME FOR THE DEATH OF A CHILD -- PROBABLY HIS SON. HE SAID THE BOY TRIED TO COPY ME BY SWINGING OFF A WAREHOUSE ATTACHED TO A PIECE OF STRING.

THE INFORMATION AS TO THE CHILD'S IDENTITY WILL BE HERE -- HIDDEN SOMEWHERE IN THE MICROFICHE READERS AT THE MIDTOWN PUBLIC LIBRARY.

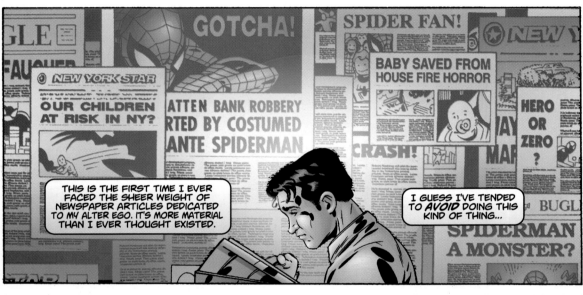

THIS IS THE FIRST TIME I EVER FACED THE SHEER WEIGHT OF NEWSPAPER ARTICLES DEDICATED TO MY ALTER EGO. IT'S MORE MATERIAL THAN I EVER THOUGHT EXISTED.

I GUESS I'VE TENDED TO *AVOID* DOING THIS KIND OF THING...

CHILD DIES IN TRAGIC ACCIDENT

By JAMES FLETCHER
STAR STAFF WRITER

Long before a wayward child playing in the shipyard district of the West Side docklands reaches the abandoned warehouses, there are signs warning of danger ahead.

For nine-year-old Jeremy Markley, these signs merely suggested a thousand potential adventures lying in wait as he attempted to emulate his favorite New York city hero; the vigilante Spider-Man. Jeremy was killed late Thursday afternoon as he attempted to swing from the top of a disused meat storage facility using a piece of string.

...DUE TO THE EXTREME LIKELIHOOD I WON'T ALWAYS BE HAPPY WITH WHAT I *FIND*.

HI. I NEED A COPY OF THIS, PLEASE.

WELL, WELL... LOOK WHO IT *AIN'T*. YOU LOOK PRETTY TICKED-OFF, PARKER.

WHAT, YOU JUST FIND OUT YOU'RE A *GEEK*, OR SOMETHING?

GOTCHA. HAD YOU WORRIED FOR A MOMENT THERE, HUH?

YEAH. LONG TIME, NO SEE, FLASH.

LUCKY YOU.

I HEARD ABOUT MARY JANE. MAN, YOU GOTTA BE THE UNLUCKIEST SAP ON THE *PLANET* AT THIS POINT.

HOW YOU GET A BABE LIKE THAT AND KEEP LOSING TRACK OF HER IS BEYOND MY COMPREHENSION --

WELL, MOST THINGS *ARE* BEYOND YOUR COMPREHENSION, FLASH. SHE WENT TO CALIFORNIA FOR A WHILE.

I *KNOW* SHE DID. LISTEN, I JUST WANTED TO SAY I KNOW IT'LL ALL WORK OUT FOR THE *BEST*, OKAY?

YOU'LL GET BY -- YOU ALWAYS *DO*.

IT'S LIKE... YOU REMEMBER WHAT HAPPENED TO JOB? I MEAN, THERE WAS ONE UNLUCKY DUDE, BUT HE KEPT ON GOING AN' IT ALL WORKED OUT IN THE END. HE LIVED TO BE A HUNDRED AND FORTY.

JOB? YOU MEAN JOB AS IN, "THE HOLY BIBLE JOB"? THE ONE WHO WAS PUT THROUGH ALL THE TRIALS?

YEAH, THAT'S THE ONE. I FIGURE YOU'RE A LOT LIKE HIM, IN A WAY. ONLY WITHOUT ALL THE DEAD COWS.

Y'KNOW, YOU NEVER CEASE TO AMAZE ME, FLASH. THERE I WAS THINKING YOU WERE AS SHALLOW AS A PUDDLE, AND YOU TURN AROUND AND PULL THIS STUFF ON ME.

I ALWAYS FIGURED THE ONLY READING YOU EVER DID WAS IN THE PAGES OF SPORTS ILLUSTRATED AND ON THE WALLS OF PUBLIC LAVATORIES.

WELL, YOU KNOW -- I BEEN DOING A LOT OF READING LATELY, TRYING TO WORK OUT SOME STUFF ABOUT MYSELF. IT'S AMAZING WHAT YOU CAN PICK UP IN A BOOK IF YOU KNOW WHERE TO LOOK.

YEAH... YEAH, IT IS.

THANKS, FLASH -- YOU ACTUALLY MADE MY DAY A LITTLE EASIER. I MEAN IT.

MY PLEASURE. YOU TAKE CARE OF YOURSELF, OKAY, PARKER?

SUCKER.

The Bible
CliffsNotes

AMAZING, ISN'T IT, HOW YOU CAN KNOW SOMEONE FOR *YEARS* AND STILL LEARN SOMETHING NEW ABOUT THEM AT ANY GIVEN MOMENT.

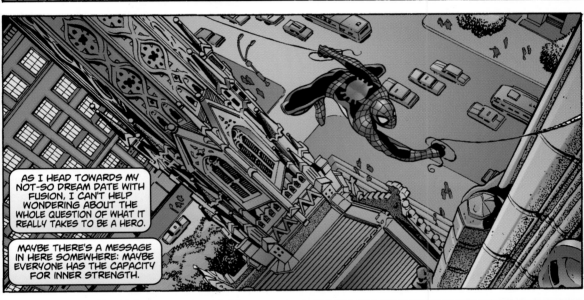

AS I HEAD TOWARDS MY NOT-SO DREAM DATE WITH *FUSION*, I CAN'T HELP WONDERING ABOUT THE WHOLE QUESTION OF WHAT IT REALLY TAKES TO BE A HERO.

MAYBE THERE'S A MESSAGE IN HERE SOMEWHERE: MAYBE EVERYONE HAS THE CAPACITY FOR INNER STRENGTH.

EVEN A GOOBER LIKE *FLASH*.

BUT THAT'S THE *POINT*, SEE? IF FLASH CAN PUT HIS DEMONS ASIDE, *ANYONE* CAN.

I'VE SEEN HIM IN HIS LOWEST MOMENTS, FIGHTING AS MUCH AGAINST *HIMSELF* AS THE ELEVATED LEVELS OF ALCOHOL IN HIS BLOODSTREAM.

COME TO THINK OF IT, FLASH AND I SHARE A COMMON EXPERIENCE IN MANY WAYS: OUR RESPECTIVE BATTLES ARE DAILY EVENTS, AFTER ALL.

YOU NEVER KNOW JUST HOW SOMEONE'S TRYING THEIR HARDEST TO DO THE RIGHT THING.

AND OF COURSE, THERE'S ALWAYS A *FLIPSIDE*.

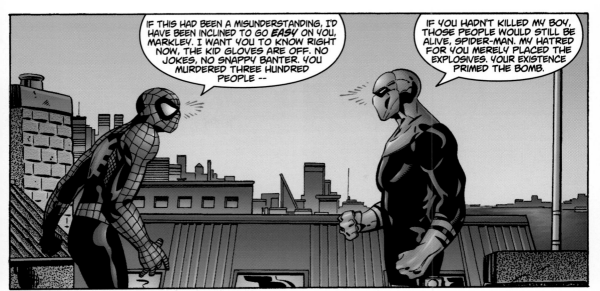

IF THIS HAD BEEN A MISUNDERSTANDING, I'D HAVE BEEN INCLINED TO GO *EASY* ON YOU, MARKLEY. I WANT YOU TO KNOW RIGHT NOW, THE KID GLOVES ARE OFF. NO JOKES, NO SNAPPY BANTER. YOU MURDERED THREE HUNDRED PEOPLE --

IF YOU HADN'T KILLED MY BOY, THOSE PEOPLE WOULD STILL BE ALIVE, SPIDER-MAN. MY HATRED FOR YOU MERELY PLACED THE EXPLOSIVES. YOUR EXISTENCE PRIMED THE BOMB.

SORRY, PAL...I'M NOT BITING. I *KNOW* PEOPLE LIKE YOU. IF I'D NEVER BEEN BORN, SOONER OR LATER, YOU WOULD'VE FOUND ANOTHER PATSY TO BLAME.

YOUR EXPERT DENIAL BELIES YOUR TRUE FEELINGS, SPIDER-MAN. YOU *KNOW* WHAT YOU TOOK FROM ME WAS MORE THAN I COULD EVER TAKE FROM YOU.

THAT'S THE KIND OF SMURF LOGIC WHICH MAKES *YOU* A VILLAIN AND *ME* A HERO.

I'M SORRY FOR WHAT HAPPENED TO YOUR SON, I TRULY AM --

LIAR!

YOU STOLE JEREMY'S LIFE, SPIDER-MAN. AND FOR THAT, *YOUR* LIFE BECOMES FORFEIT --

SLAM

AA-UHH!

OOOOW!

...HHH...LISTEN TO ME, MARKLEY...IT NEVER HAD TO *BE* THIS WAY. IT COULD ALWAYS HAVE BEEN DIFFERENT --

WHAT DO *YOU* KNOW, YOU TIRED EXCUSE FOR A HUMAN BEING? YOU DON'T KNOW MY MIND...

...AND YOU DON'T KNOW MY *HEART* --!

WHAM

UHH...I KNOW YOU BETTER THAN YOU *THINK*, PAL. YOU FIT THE MOLD PERFECTLY: ALL YOUR ANGER'S DRIVEN BY A SERIES OF CONVENIENT *EXCUSES* --

SHUT UP! I'LL *KILL* YOU!

BURN.

SHOOM

AAH!

~AH-HUHH~ EASIER TO SCREAM THAN TO *THINK*, HUH, FUSION?

WHACK

WELL, WELL... AS THEY SAY: EVERY DOG HAS HIS DAY. YOU JUST HAD YOURS.

COME ON, THEN, DOUGHBOY. LET'S SEE IF YOU'VE GOT WHAT IT TAKES TO *SWING* A LITTLE.

YOU'RE MERELY PROLONGING THE INEVITABLE, SPIDER-MAN. I CAN FOLLOW YOU WHEREVER YOU GO.

BUT I AM *FASTER* --

-- AND I WANT YOU DEAD MORE THAN YOU WANT TO BE *ALIVE*.

THWIP

BOOM

UHNN--!

I'M BEGINNING TO WONDER IF HE ISN'T *RIGHT*: I'VE BEEN AROUND ENOUGH OF THESE SUPERLOONS TO KNOW WHEN I MIGHT BE FIGHTING A LOSING BATTLE.

HE'S QUICKER THAN LIGHTNING. FEELS LIKE I'M WEARING LEAD WEIGHTS IN COMPARISON.

UHH!

CRASH

MM. I'D HOPED TO GAIN SOME SMALL SATISFACTION FROM THIS MOMENT, SPIDER-MAN. BUT YOU'VE PROVEN TO BE A MILD DISAPPOINTMENT AT BEST.

I SHOULD HAVE *KNOWN* YOU WOULDN'T HAVE THE PASSION FOR THIS CONFLICT THAT I DID --

...NNN...KEEP IT UP, DILLWEED. I...I GOT THREE HUNDRED REASONS TO PROVE YOU WRONG...

DON'T EXPECT ME TO BE IMPRESSED -- YOU DIDN'T STAND A CHANCE THE MOMENT YOU ARRIVED.

YOU'RE IN NO CONDITION TO CONTINUE, SPIDER-MAN, YET YOU CARRY ON REGARDLESS. I COMMEND YOU FOR YOUR STUBBORN ATTACHMENT TO A LIFE OF *FUTILITY*.

BUT YOU ARE ALREADY FINISHED. YOU'RE NOTHING AGAINST THE MIGHT OF MY POWERS.

WHAT IF YOU HAD TO FACE THE HULK... WHAT WOULD YOU DO THEN?

WHAT IF THE HULK COULD MOVE WITH THE SPEED OF QUICKSILVER...

...OR WAS ABLE TO DISTORT REALITY LIKE MYSTERIO?

WHAT IF YOUR ADVERSARY HAD ALL THOSE POWERS, SPIDER-MAN...

...AND COULD BECOME *INVISIBLE*?

UHH...YOU REALLY THINK THIS MAKES A *DIFFERENCE*, FUSION? TIME TO STOP KIDDING YOURSELF.

IF JEREMY HADN'T DIVED OFF THE BUILDING, WHAT'S THE BETTING IT WOULD HAVE BEEN MOMMY'S DRINKING OR THAT TIME DADDY TOOK AWAY ALL OF YOUR TOYS --

BEHIND YOU, CRETIN.

HH-AHH!

WHAT'S WRONG, SPIDER-MAN? HAVING TROUBLE SEEING STRAIGHT?

I CAN'T...GET A HANDLE ON THIS GUY. SOMEHOW, HE CAN AFFECT MY SPIDER-SENSE.

I KEEP THINKING I'VE *GOT* HIM, AND THEN...

...AND THEN, YOU *LOSE*.

WHACKO

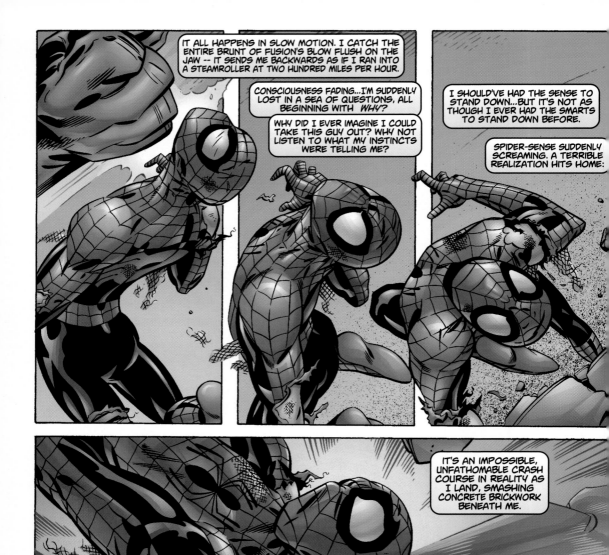

IT ALL HAPPENS IN SLOW MOTION. I CATCH THE ENTIRE BRUNT OF FUSION'S BLOW FLUSH ON THE JAW -- IT SENDS ME BACKWARDS AS IF I RAN INTO A STEAMROLLER AT TWO HUNDRED MILES PER HOUR.

CONSCIOUSNESS FADING...I'M SUDDENLY LOST IN A SEA OF QUESTIONS, ALL BEGINNING WITH *WHY*?

WHY DID I EVER IMAGINE I COULD TAKE THIS GUY OUT? WHY NOT LISTEN TO WHAT MY INSTINCTS WERE TELLING ME?

I SHOULD'VE HAD THE SENSE TO STAND DOWN...BUT IT'S NOT AS THOUGH I EVER HAD THE SMARTS TO STAND DOWN BEFORE.

SPIDER-SENSE SUDDENLY SCREAMING. A TERRIBLE REALIZATION HITS HOME:

IT'S AN IMPOSSIBLE, UNFATHOMABLE CRASH COURSE IN REALITY AS I LAND, SMASHING CONCRETE BRICKWORK BENEATH ME.

I KNOW WITH UTMOST CERTAINTY THIS IS ONE TIME I'M GOING TO *HAVE* TO ADMIT DEFEAT.

I'M NOT GOING TO BE ABLE TO STAND AND FACE FUSION AGAIN. NOT *THIS* TIME.

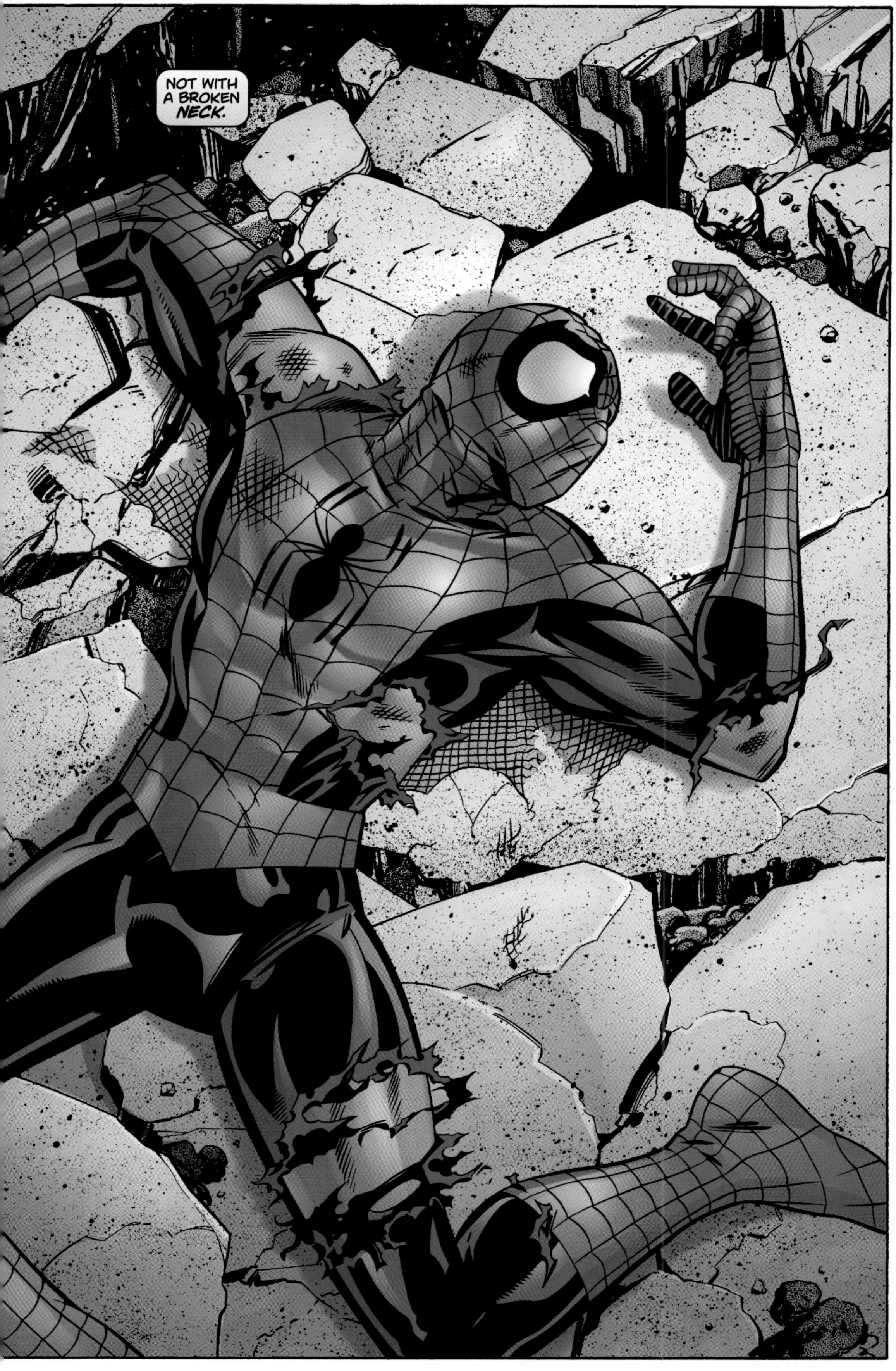
NOT WITH A BROKEN NECK.

I WAKE ON COLD STONE, HEARING A SINGLE SOUND REPEATED OVER AND OVER AGAIN, AS IF IT'S COMING FROM A DREAM:

SNAP.

WHUD

≥UKK≤

SNAP. THE BRUTAL TRUTH OF IT CLATTERS LIKE A DRILL HAMMER ON MY MIND: "END OF THE LINE, WEB-SLINGER -- BROKEN NECK... BETTER LUCK NEXT TIME."

IT'S AS MUCH AS I CAN DO TO BREATHE. THAT CRASHING SOUND IS THE SOUND OF MY FUTURE, SHATTERED. IT'S ALL OVER.

I'LL NEVER WALK AGAIN.

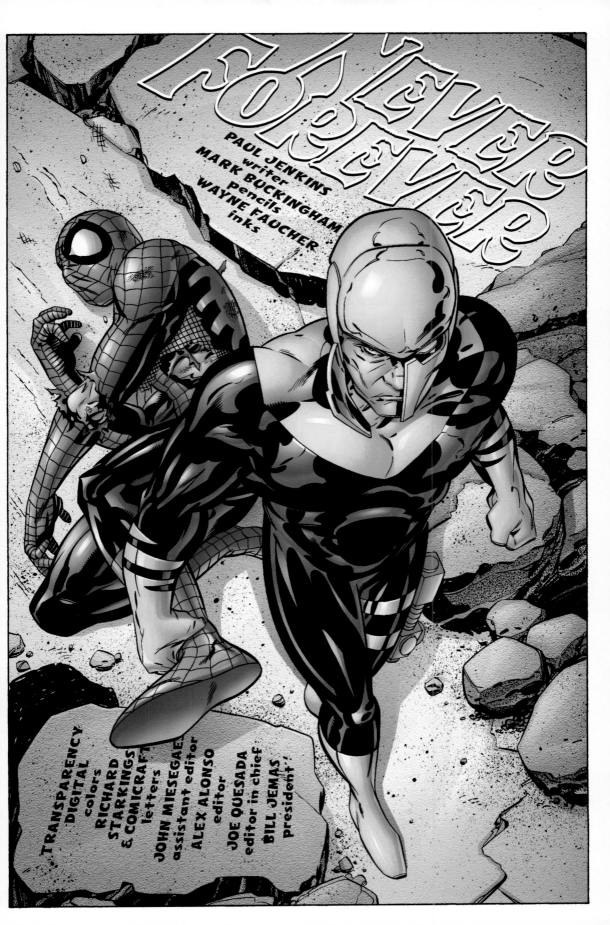

FOREVER

PAUL JENKINS
writer
MARK BUCKINGHAM
pencils
WAYNE FAUCHER
inks

TRANSPARENCY
DIGITAL
colors
RICHARD
STARKINGS
& COMICRAFT
letters
JOHN MIESEGAES
assistant editor
ALEX ALONSO
editor
JOE QUESADA
editor in chief
BILL JEMAS
president!

THE GREAT SPIDER-MAN -- BANE OF THE CRIMINAL SET -- CUT DOWN IN HIS PRIME: *OH, HOW THE SINGLE MOTHERS OF MANHATTAN WILL WEEP WHEN THEY HEAR THE NEWS.*

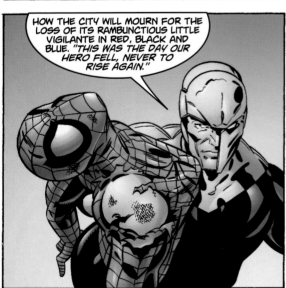

HOW THE CITY WILL MOURN FOR THE LOSS OF ITS RAMBUNCTIOUS LITTLE VIGILANTE IN RED, BLACK AND BLUE. *"THIS WAS THE DAY OUR HERO FELL, NEVER TO RISE AGAIN."*

BUT TOMORROW, THEY'LL MOURN YOU A LITTLE *LESS,* SPIDER-MAN.

≥HUFF≤

THE PAIN WILL GO AWAY, A DIFFERENT HERO WILL COME TO TAKE YOUR PLACE...

...AND BY NEXT WEEK YOU'LL FADE INTO A FOND *REMEMBRANCE.*

NO ONE WILL UNDERSTAND WHAT HAPPENED HERE TODAY. NO ONE WILL CARE.

NO ONE...

"...BUT YOU."

I KNOW WHAT YOU'RE THINKING.

YOU'RE THINKING ABOUT ALL THOSE *PEOPLE* WHO DIED. YOUR NECK IS BROKEN...YOU'RE BEYOND HOPE, COMPLETELY AT MY MERCY.

BUT YOU CAN'T *HELP* YOURSELF, CAN YOU?

HERE'S A LITTLE POISONED FOOD FOR THOUGHT FOR YOU TO CHOKE ON: THE BOMB THAT BLEW UP THE EDGAR BUILDING WOULD NEVER HAVE EXPLODED IF *YOU* HADN'T STOPPED IT FROM FALLING.

THE DEVICE WAS WIRED TO AN ALTIMETER, PRIMED TO DETONATE IF THE NEEDLE STOPPED BEFORE IT REACHED ZERO. IF IT HAD BEEN ALLOWED TO FALL, IT WOULD HAVE LANDED HARMLESSLY.

BUT INSTEAD *YOU* STEPPED IN TO SAVE THE DAY. *THINK* ABOUT IT, SPIDER-MAN:

>UKK<

CRASH

THREE HUNDRED PEOPLE ARE DEAD BECAUSE YOU CHOSE TO BE A *HERO*.

LYING ON THE FLOOR OF FUSION'S HIDEOUT, I TRY TO MAKE SENSE OF WHAT'S HAPPENED.

BUT I *CAN'T*.

CAN'T HEAR MYSELF THINK. CAN'T MOVE MY FINGERS. IF I COULD JUST...

I'M SUPPOSED TO *BE* SOMEWHERE -- I PROMISED CARYN I'D FEED BARKER. HE'LL BE WAITING. *HUNGRY.*

IF SHE FINDS OUT I DIDN'T FEED HIM, SHE'LL FREAK. I DON'T KNOW WHAT I'M GOING TO SAY WHEN I...

DON'T KNOW IF I'LL EVER...I'LL NEVER...

MOVE.

NO...THIS *CAN'T* BE RIGHT -- I MUST'VE *FORGOTTEN* SOMETHING. DID I LEAVE THE FRIDGE DOOR OPEN?

CARROTS. THAT'S IT... I DIDN'T PICK UP ANY *CARROTS.* I NEVER EAT CARROTS.

NEVER.

I'LL NEVER...

I'LL NEVER WALK *AGAIN.*

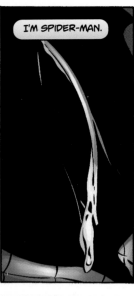

I'M SPIDER-MAN.

I CAN'T GIVE UP.

I'VE GOT TO...*TRY.*

GOT TO FOCUS... ON SOMETHING ELSE.

JONAH -- WHAT'S HE DOING RIGHT NOW? CHEWING SOMEONE OUT, PROBABLY.

HEHH... UH...

MAYBE IT'S JUST TEMPORARY.

COME ON...MOVE, DAMN YOU. *MOVE.*

PLEASE.

PLEASE MOVE.

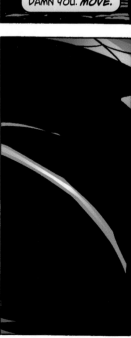

AN IMAGE APPEARS IN MY MIND'S EYE...A MEMORY OF THE FUTURE, IF SUCH A THING IS POSSIBLE. IT'S LIKE I REMEMBER AN IMPOSSIBLE SECRET THAT SOMEONE ONCE TOLD ME...

...IS THIS ME?

WHAT'S HAPPENING TO ME? WHERE'S FUSION -- WHY DIDN'T HE COME BACK?

WHY DOESN'T HE...?

MOVE!

MARY JANE'S GOING TO BE SO SCARED WHEN SHE FINDS OUT.

I MISS HER SO MUCH.

WHAT IF SHE DOESN'T FIND OUT? WHAT IF I DIE HERE?

WHAT IF I NEVER...

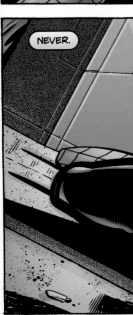

NEVER.

WALK.

AGAIN.

I DON'T WANT TO KNOW WHO YOU ARE UNDER THAT MASK. I DON'T WANT TO KNOW THAT YOU HAVE A FACE.

YOU'RE NOT A *PERSON* TO ME.

...HHH... WHHHYY...?

BECAUSE OF *YOU*. BECAUSE YOU FANCIED YOURSELF A PUBLIC SERVANT, BUT YOU COULDN'T CUT IT.

YOU COULDN'T EVEN SAVE ONE LITTLE BOY.

...WASN'T... MY... ...FAULT...

AND BECAUSE YOU ARE A LIAR.

YOU WERE SUPPOSED TO BE A FORCE FOR GOOD, SPIDER-MAN --

-- A BEACON OF BRAVERY WHERE ALL AROUND YOU WAS DARK.

BUT YOU LOST YOUR WAY. YOU FORGOT THAT SELF-IMPOSED EDICT OF YOURS: SERVE AND PROTECT.

MY FRANCIS WAS JUST A LITTLE BOY WHO RELIED ON THE HELP OF HIS HERO. YOU BROKE HIS TRUST.

WHAT DO YOU THINK WENT THROUGH MY SON'S MIND AS THE STRING SNAPPED AND HE PLUMMETED TO EARTH, SPIDER-MAN? DO YOU THINK HE WONDERED WHERE YOU WERE?

EVEN AS HIS SHATTERED LITTLE FRAME HIT THE GROUND, DID HE STILL BELIEVE YOU WERE GOING TO SAVE HIM?

OR DO YOU THINK HIS HEART HAD ALREADY DIED, REALIZING YOU'D NEGLECTED YOUR DUTY TO HIM?

KEEP SHOUTIN' AN' MAYBE YOU WON'T HEAR THE SOUND OF YOUR OWN GUILT.

WHAT? WHAT DID YOU SAY?

...HHH... I SAID... "KEEP SHOUTIN'..."

"AN' MAYBE YOU WON'T HEAR..."

"...THE SOUND OF YOUR OWN GUILT..."

HRAHH!

CRASH

-GUHH-

IS THERE A CODE OF ETHICS, YOU FOOL? IS THERE A STANDARD BY WHICH YOUR ADVERSARIES TREAT YOU --

-- WHEN THEY HAVE YOU PRISONER?

WHACK

WELL, I DON'T NEED TO PLAY BY THE RULES OF YOUR SAD LITTLE GAME, SPIDER-MAN. YOU DIDN'T PLAY BY THE RULES OF MINE.

SO LISTEN TO ME, AND LISTEN WELL: YOU'RE FINISHED.

YOUR NECK IS BROKEN. YOU'LL NEVER WALK AGAIN.

I HOPE IT BURNS ON YOUR HEART FOREVER.

FOREVER. I'M GOING TO BE STUCK LIKE THIS FOREVER.

I'VE BEEN THROUGH A MILLION LEVELS OF DESPAIR, BUT NONE LIKE *THIS*. THERE'S NOTHING I CAN DO.

I'LL NEVER WALK AGAIN. I *CAN'T*...

I CAN'T MOVE MY FINGERS. I CAN'T *THINK* STRAIGHT.

MY SPIDER SENSES... WHY DIDN'T THEY *WARN* ME ABOUT THE BOMB?

THERE'S SOMETHING *WRONG* WITH THAT, SPIDEY -- *THINK!*

I'M SUPPOSED TO BE A HERO. I'M SUPPOSED TO *FIGHT*.

FIGHT!

I DON'T LOSE.

THAT'S NOT WHO I *AM*.

I NEVER...

NEVER.

GIVE.

UP.

...HNN... -EHH-

CLANG

WHAT --?

IS THAT A COUPLE OF *GRAPES* IN YOUR SPANDEX, FUSION...

...UHH...

...OR ARE YOU JUST SURPRISED TO *SEE* ME?

YOU CAN'T BE STANDING. YOU BROKE YOUR NECK.

MAYBE I DID...HHH...OR MAYBE...

...MAYBE THAT'S JUST WHAT YOU WANT ME...TO *THINK*...

NO! STAY *BACK!*

AH-UHH...!

YOUR NECK IS BROKEN, SPIDER-MAN -- YOU ARE PARALYZED. STOP TRYING TO CONVINCE YOURSELF OTHERWISE.

YOU DON'T STAND A CHANCE AGAINST ME. YOU'VE *LOST.*

YEAH, WELL...HHH...I DON'T *THINK* SO.

I THINK...YOU DON'T REALLY HAVE ALL THAT POWER. I THINK IT'S JUST AUTOSUGGESTION. YOU'RE JUST A POOR MAN'S MYSTERIO...

...AN' I JUST FIGURED YOU *OUT.*

VERY WELL THEN, SPIDER-MAN. HAVE IT *YOUR* WAY.

SMASH

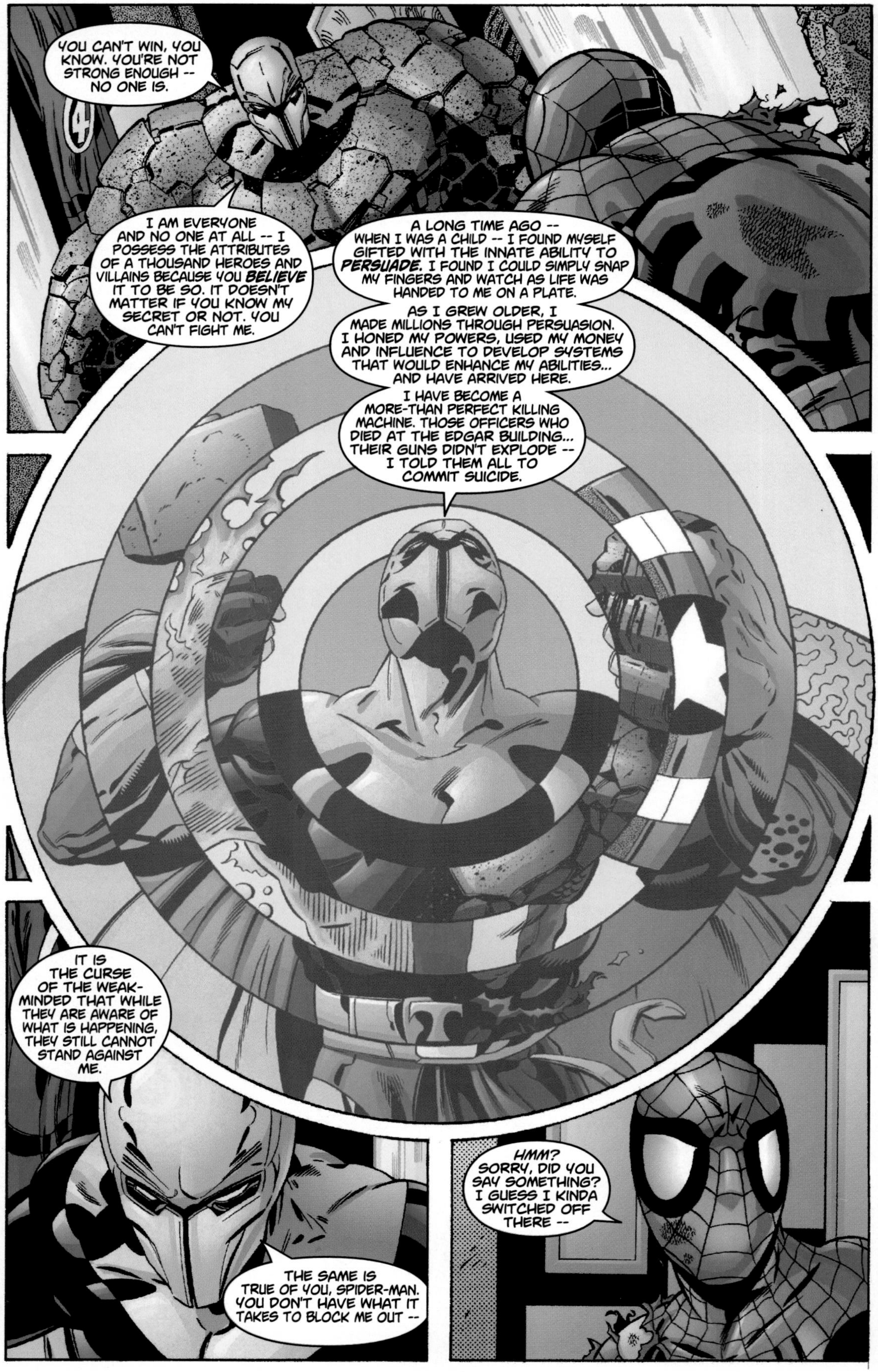
YOU CAN'T WIN, YOU KNOW. YOU'RE NOT STRONG ENOUGH -- NO ONE IS.
I AM EVERYONE AND NO ONE AT ALL -- I POSSESS THE ATTRIBUTES OF A THOUSAND HEROES AND VILLAINS BECAUSE YOU *BELIEVE* IT TO BE SO. IT DOESN'T MATTER IF YOU KNOW MY SECRET OR NOT. YOU CAN'T FIGHT ME.
A LONG TIME AGO -- WHEN I WAS A CHILD -- I FOUND MYSELF GIFTED WITH THE INNATE ABILITY TO *PERSUADE.* I FOUND I COULD SIMPLY SNAP MY FINGERS AND WATCH AS LIFE WAS HANDED TO ME ON A PLATE.
AS I GREW OLDER, I MADE MILLIONS THROUGH PERSUASION. I HONED MY POWERS, USED MY MONEY AND INFLUENCE TO DEVELOP SYSTEMS THAT WOULD ENHANCE MY ABILITIES... AND HAVE ARRIVED HERE.
I HAVE BECOME A MORE-THAN PERFECT KILLING MACHINE. THOSE OFFICERS WHO DIED AT THE EDGAR BUILDING... THEIR GUNS DIDN'T EXPLODE -- I TOLD THEM ALL TO COMMIT SUICIDE.
IT IS THE CURSE OF THE WEAK-MINDED THAT WHILE THEY ARE AWARE OF WHAT IS HAPPENING, THEY STILL CANNOT STAND AGAINST ME.
THE SAME IS TRUE OF YOU, SPIDER-MAN. YOU DON'T HAVE WHAT IT TAKES TO BLOCK ME OUT --
HMM? SORRY, DID YOU SAY SOMETHING? I GUESS I KINDA SWITCHED OFF THERE --

YOU **WILL** PAY HEED, SPIDER-MAN -- YOU CAN NO MORE FIGHT MY POWERS OF SUGGESTION THAN A DAISY COULD STOP AN ARMORED CAR.

YOU KNOW ME TO BE FUSION, BUT YOUR SENSES TELL YOU IT IS DOCTOR OCTOPUS WHO FACES YOU THIS MOMENT.

YOU'RE LOSING YOUR TOUCH, FUSION -- OL' DOC OCK'S A LOT FASTER THAN THAT!

PLUS, HE'S A CERTS WITH RETSIN MAN...

WHACK

GUHH!

SMASSH

...YOU SMELL LIKE A LISTERINE KINDA GUY --

DOOM.

YOW!

ZZAKT

HAMMER.

SORRY, PAL -- NOT THIS TIME.

THWIP

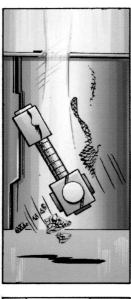

NO... IT CAN'T BE --

SAY, DID ANYONE LOSE A LITTLE SQUARE DOOHICKEY? I THINK IT'S PART OF SOMEONE'S OLD, CLAPPED-OUT MASTER PLAN --

DETONATE. CODE.. ALPHA-NINE-THETA --

UH-OH.

THOOM

AW, CRUD --

YEAH, THAT'S IT -- NOT SO TOUGH WITHOUT YOUR DOOHICKEY, ARE YOU?

TELL YOU WHAT: JUST FOR LAUGHS, I'LL GIVE YOU A TEN SECOND HEAD-START.

TIME'S UP!

OH, LOOK: THERE HE IS!

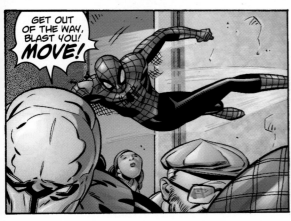

GET OUT OF THE WAY, BLAST YOU! MOVE!

YEAH... THAT'S WHAT THEY ALL SAY IN THE END --

WHACK

HHH... ONE!

STOP ME WHEN I GET TO THREE HUNDRED, YOU &'@#*!

NO! YOU WILL NOT DEFEAT ME!

DIE.

WHUMP

NO.

YOU CAN'T DEFEAT ME... YOU CAN'T...

...IT'S NOT POSSIBLE...

YOU LOST THE MOMENT YOU SET EYES ON ME, MARKLEY. YOU BEAT YOURSELF... IT WAS ALWAYS YOUR OWN LACK OF HEROISM YOU DESPISED.

BUT YOU'RE TOO FULL OF SELF-LOATHING TO SEE IT, AREN'T YOU? THE DIFFERENCE BETWEEN YOU AND ME IS STRENGTH OF WILL.

FOR JUST A MOMENT YOU HAD ME BELIEVING THAT IT WAS ME WHO KILLED THREE HUNDRED PEOPLE. BUT THEY DIED BECAUSE YOU'RE A COWARD --

CRASH.

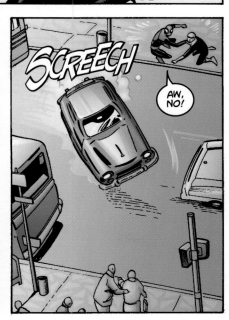

SCREECH

AW, NO!

HEADS UP, PEOPLE! COMING THROUGH!

≥HH-UHH!≤

SCREEE

MARKLEY!

A BROKEN NECK -- REAL OR IMAGINED -- IS THE SORT OF THING CAN GIVE YOU A SENSE OF CLARITY.

LOOKING AT TODAY'S EVENTS FROM A DISTANCE, I CAN SEE HOW MARKLEY USED THE DEATH OF HIS SON AS AN EXCUSE TO MAIM AND KILL.

I TOOK WHAT HAPPENED TO MY UNCLE BEN AND USED IT AS MY CATALYST FOR SPIDER-MAN. SAME PROBLEM, DIFFERENT EXCUSE, I GUESS.

SO, WHAT HAVE WE LEARNED FROM TODAY'S LESSON..?

SNIFF SNIFF

HERE YA GO, BARKS... DON'T FORGET TO CHEW.

SLAP

SNRFF

...THAT THERE'S A FINE LINE BETWEEN HERO AND PSYCHO, I GUESS.

END

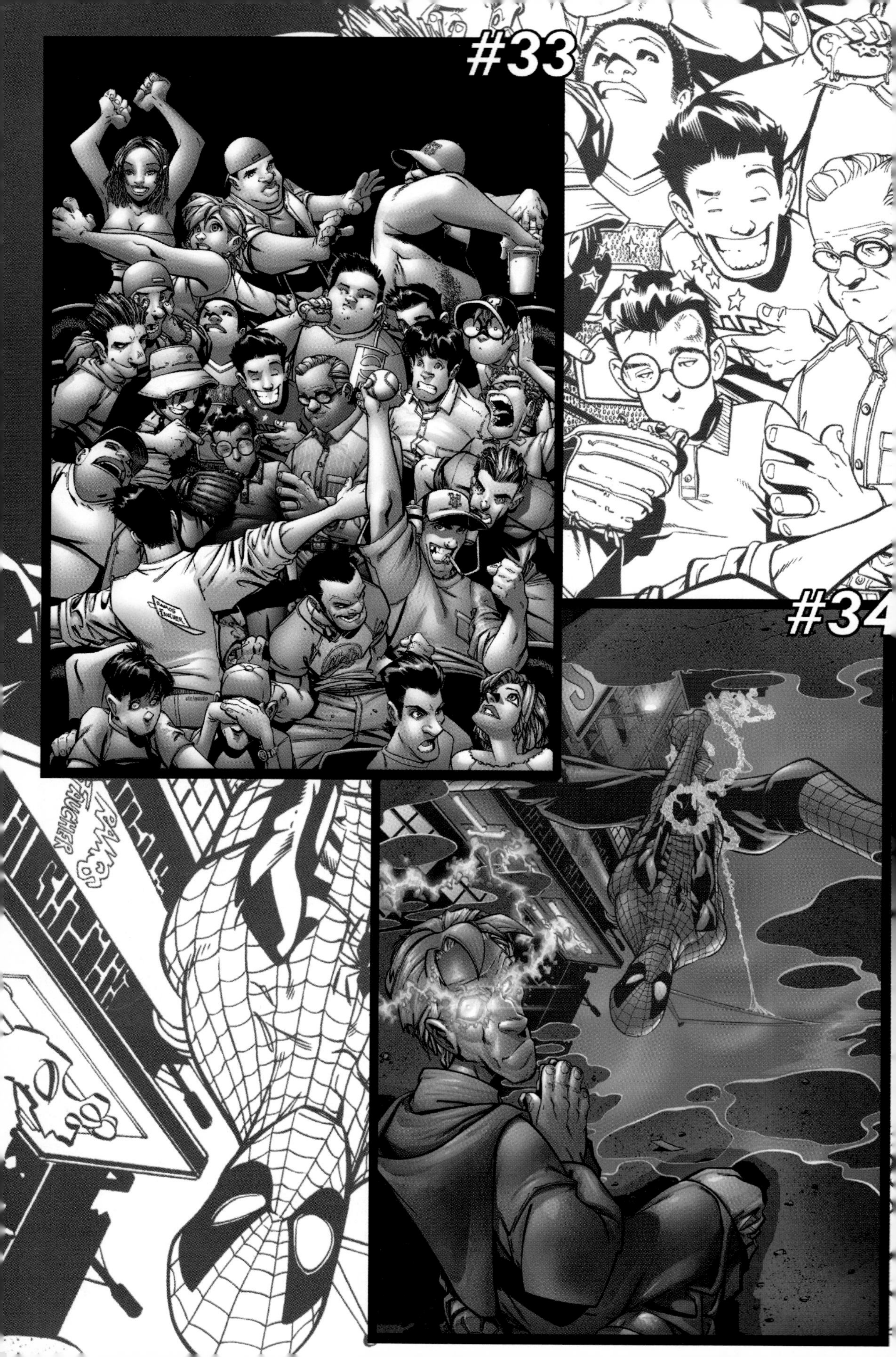
#33
#34

WHEN I WAS A KID, TIME WAS A SNAIL.

NOW, IT'S A *GREYHOUND*.

BUCKY + WAYNE ④

EVERY YEAR, THIS DAY COMES AROUND...REGULARLY LIKE CLOCKWORK AND MORE *QUICKLY* THAN THE YEAR BEFORE.

I ALWAYS KNOW IT'S COMING, BUT IT NEVER FAILS TO TAKE ME BY SURPRISE.

THIS IS THE DAY MY UNCLE BEN DIED.

I REMEMBER MORE WEIRD LITTLE MINUTIAE THAN ANYTHING ELSE. AUNT MAY WAS MAKING PEACH COBBLER THAT NIGHT. I WAS SHUFFLING HOME WITH MY HANDS IN MY POCKETS, THINKING ABOUT SUPERMODELS.

AS I TURNED THE CORNER TO OUR HOUSE, I SAW FLASHING LIGHTS AND A COUPLE OF NEIGHBORS OUT IN THE STREET. FOR A MOMENT, I THOUGHT MAYBE A GAS MAIN HAD BROKEN. BUT IT WAS SOMETHING MUCH, MUCH *WORSE*.

UNCLE BEN LAY AT THE FOOT OF THE STAIRS, HIS FACE ASHEN WHITE AND STIFF, HIS BLOOD POOLING OUT LIKE A BIG RED STARFISH, THE POLICE WERE ASKING AUNT MAY QUESTIONS NEXT DOOR.

I REMEMBER ONE OF THE DETECTIVES LATER ASKED ME IF I'D SEEN ANYONE SUSPICIOUS, AND I JUST *LOST* IT. WHAT WAS I GOING TO SAY? "YES, DETECTIVE. I HAVE THE POWERS OF A LARGE SPIDER, AND YOU KNOW THE GUY WHO MURDERED THE ONLY FATHER I EVER KNEW? I LET HIM ESCAPE JUST LAST WEEK."

UNCLE BEN ALWAYS USED TO SAY HOW WITH GREAT POWER CAME GREAT RESPONSIBILITY--I GUESS I TOOK HIM PRETTY *LITERALLY* ON THAT ONE. I FOUND MYSELF FIGHTING BAD GUYS WHO ALWAYS SEEMED TO BE IN NEED OF A HAIRCUT OR A NEW WARDROBE. BUT I NEVER LOST SIGHT OF WHY I WAS DOING IT IN THE FIRST PLACE.

BEN PA
HE V
LOV

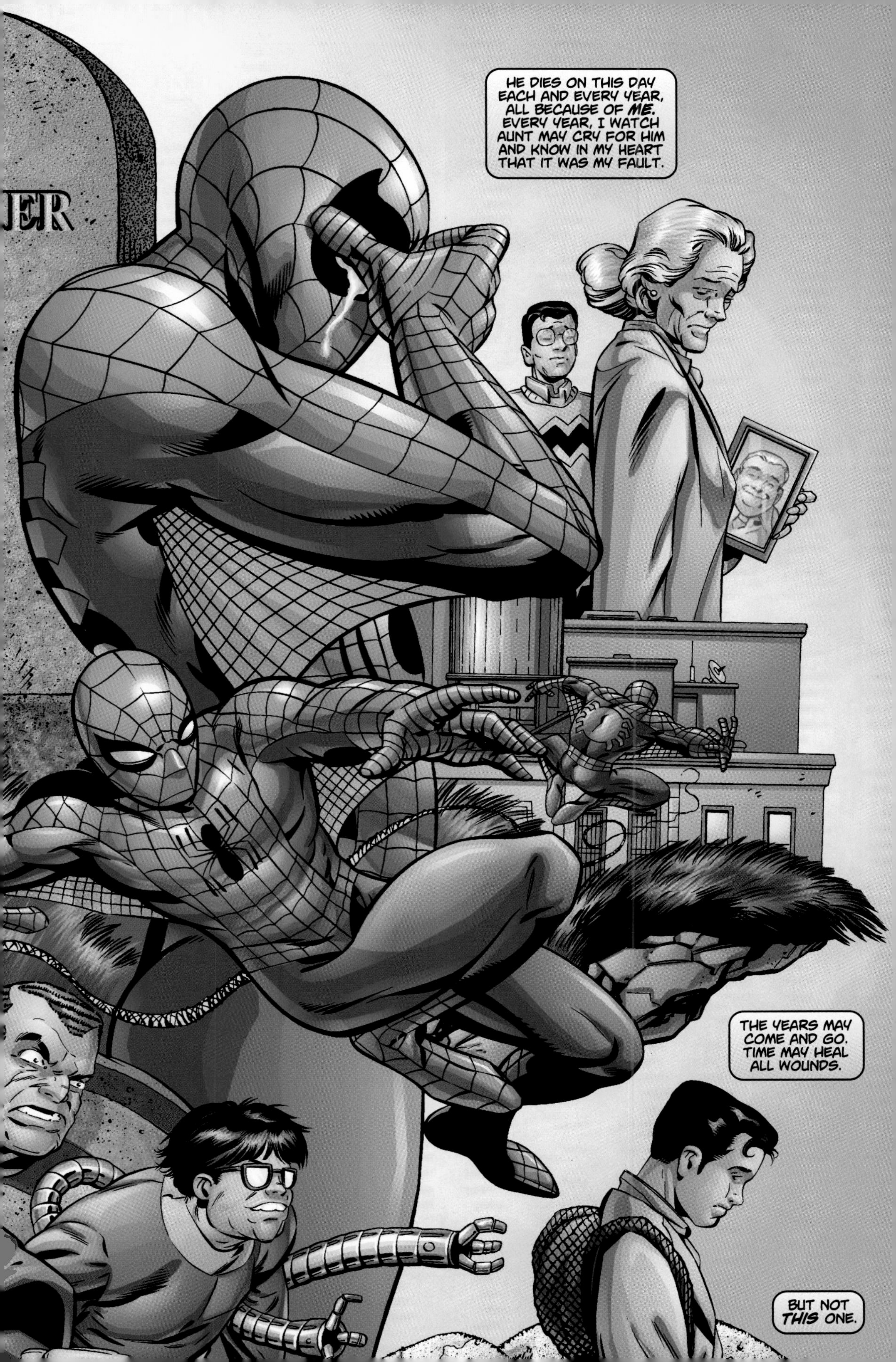
HE DIES ON THIS DAY EACH AND EVERY YEAR, ALL BECAUSE OF ME. EVERY YEAR, I WATCH AUNT MAY CRY FOR HIM AND KNOW IN MY HEART THAT IT WAS MY FAULT.
JER
THE YEARS MAY COME AND GO. TIME MAY HEAL ALL WOUNDS.
BUT NOT THIS ONE.

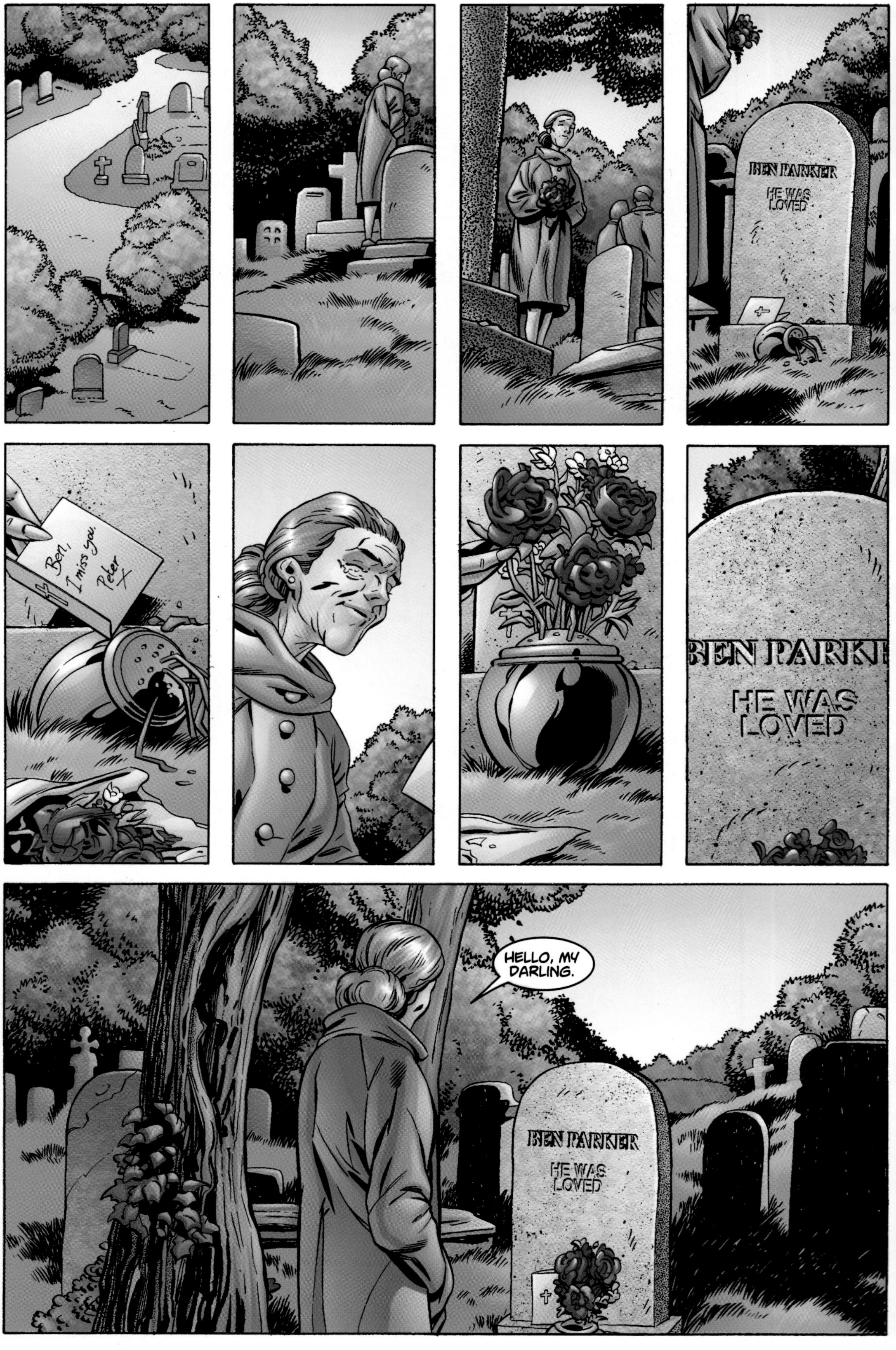
BEN PARKER
HE WAS LOVED
Ben,
I miss you.
Peter
X
BEN PARKE
HE WAS LOVED
HELLO, MY DARLING.
BEN PARKER
HE WAS LOVED

I NEVER *GO* WITH HER... NOT BECAUSE OF *GUILT*, BUT BECAUSE I FIGURE SHE NEEDS TO BE ALONE WITH HIM ONCE IN A WHILE. SHE MISSES HIM AS MUCH NOW AS SHE *EVER* DID.

SOMETIMES, I GET THE IMPRESSION SHE'S JUST BIDING HER TIME, SEEING ME THROUGH A FEW MORE YEARS BEFORE SHE GOES OFF TO VISIT WITH THE GOOD OLD BOY FOR GOOD.

IT'S BEEN HARD TO MAKE PEACE WITH MYSELF, KNOWING WHAT I KNOW. I GUESS YOU COULD SAY MY REDEMPTION IS A WORK IN PROGRESS.

I'M STILL *TRYING*, THOUGH. WHEN THE ANNIVERSARY ROLLS AROUND, I HAVE MY OWN PARTICULAR WAY OF DEALING WITH IT.

I GO WITH A FINE OLD PARKER FAMILY *TRADITION*.

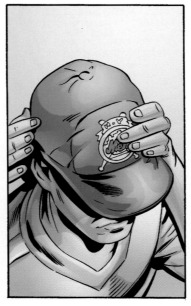

YOU *READY*, BOSS?

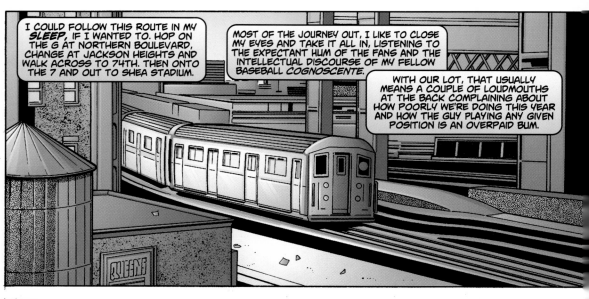

I COULD FOLLOW THIS ROUTE IN MY *SLEEP*, IF I WANTED TO. HOP ON THE G AT NORTHERN BOULEVARD, CHANGE AT JACKSON HEIGHTS AND WALK ACROSS TO 74TH. THEN ONTO THE 7 AND OUT TO SHEA STADIUM.

MOST OF THE JOURNEY OUT, I LIKE TO CLOSE MY EYES AND TAKE IT ALL IN, LISTENING TO THE EXPECTANT HUM OF THE FANS AND THE INTELLECTUAL DISCOURSE OF MY FELLOW BASEBALL *COGNOSCENTE.*

WITH OUR LOT, THAT USUALLY MEANS A COUPLE OF LOUDMOUTHS AT THE BACK COMPLAINING ABOUT HOW POORLY WE'RE DOING THIS YEAR AND HOW THE GUY PLAYING ANY GIVEN POSITION IS AN OVERPAID BUM.

I GUESS I COULD ALWAYS *IDENTIFY* WITH THE METS, YOU KNOW? A BUNCH OF LOVABLE LOSERS WHO HIT THE OCCASIONAL HOME RUN BY ACCIDENT. JUST LIKE ME.

AS WE RATTLE AND HUM ON OUR WAY TO THE GAME, THE AIR'S A MIXTURE OF SWEAT, TOBACCO RESIDUE AND *HOPE.* EVERYONE'S AS DESPERATE AS ME FOR A HOT DOG AND A *WIN.*

BY THE TIME WE GET TO WILLETS POINT, THE CROWD IS A SEA OF BLUE. THIS IS MY TEAM, MY EXTENDED FAMILY OF MISFITS.

ME AND AMERICAN TRADITION: WHAT A *PAIR.*

IT'S A SHORT WALK TO SHEA FROM HERE. YOU CAN IMAGINE RED SOX OR CUB FANS MAKING THE SAME TRIP TODAY, DOOMED AND EXPECTANT AT THE SAME TIME.

THAT TIME IN '86 WHEN BILLY BUCK LET THAT GROUND BALL THROUGH HIS LEGS, YOU DIDN'T KNOW WHETHER TO LAUGH OR *CRY.* I FIGURE THERE'S SOME OLD DUDE IN BOSTON STILL GAPING SLACK-JAWED AT THE TV SCREEN, MUTTERING ABOUT THE *"CURSE OF THE BAMBINO"* AND WONDERING IF BUCKNER'LL FIELD IT CLEANLY ON THE REPLAY.

THAT WORLD SERIES WAS JUST A BLIP ON THE RADAR SCREEN OF FATE FOR US, I GUESS. AFTER THAT, WE REJOINED THE RANK AND FILE, WHILE THE OTHER GUYS CONTINUED TO RACK UP DIAMOND RINGS AND MEDIA ATTENTION AT THE RICH END OF TOWN.

BUT TO ME, IT'S NEVER BEEN ABOUT WINNING. BASEBALL'S FAR BIGGER THAN JUST A GOOD RESULT.

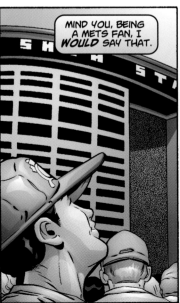

MIND YOU, BEING A METS FAN, I *WOULD* SAY THAT.

WHAT D'YOU SAY, UNCLE BEN? MAYBE *THIS* YEAR?

TURNSTILE.

TURNSTILE AGAIN.

C'MON PETEY... WE'RE IN THE FAN CLUB SEATS JUST BEHIND THE DUGOUT.

MEGA!

THE FIRST TIME HE BROUGHT ME HERE, I HAD NO IDEA WHAT TO EXPECT. HECK, THE FACT THAT WE'D JUST RIDDEN THE SUBWAY WAS MORE THAN I COULD'VE EXPECTED OUT OF MY AFTERNOON.

UNCLE BEN HAD GOTTEN OUR TICKETS FROM MISTER WATSON DOWN AT THE CORNER STORE. HE FIGURED IT WAS HIGH TIME I LEARNED THE FINER POINTS OF BASEBALL.

ME, I COULD HAVE CARED LESS ABOUT BATTING AVERAGES. I WANTED TO KNOW ABOUT THE REALLY *COOL* STUFF --

WHATTA THEM BIG NUMBERS FOR, UNCA BEN?

THOSE ARE RETIRED JERSEYS--

WHASSA BIG APPLE FOR?

FOR WHEN WE HIT A HOME RUN--

C'N WE BUY WUNNA THEM BIG, POINTY FINGUZ?

SURE WE CAN.

THERE ARE SOME PRETTY GOOD SEATS, HUH, KILLER? YOU EXCITED?

UH-HUH. *YEAH!*

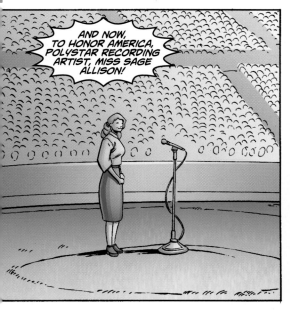

AND NOW, TO HONOR AMERICA, POLYSTAR RECORDING ARTIST, MISS SAGE ALLISON!

♪ OHHH, SAY CAN YOU SEEE... ♪

ALL OF *THREE* SECONDS...THAT'S HOW LONG IT TOOK ME TO FALL UNDER BASEBALL'S SPELL.

IMMEDIATELY, I WAS *CAPTIVATED.* FROM MY SECRET PERCH ABOVE AND LEFT OF HOME PLATE, I WATCHED IN EARNEST AS THE MOST PROFOUND DRAMA IN ALL OF HUMAN HISTORY UNFOLDED BEFORE ME.

I'D NEVER SEEN ANYONE THROW A FASTBALL BEFORE. IT WAS LIKE WATCHING A GUY TRY TO FEND OFF A BULLET WITH A PLASTIC STRAW.

SAFE!

WHROOOOSH

NEXT THING YOU KNOW, THE CROWD AROUND ME HAD DISSOLVED INTO AN AMORPHOUS BLOB OF BLUE. I WAS DOWN THERE ON THE FIELD WITH MY NEWFOUND HEROES...

...THE OTHER TEAM'S MANAGER WAS SCREAMING AT AN OFFICIAL OVER A BAD CALL...

...THE BATTER HAD TWO STRIKES. THE PITCHER WAS BEGINNING HIS WIND-UP...

...AND ME, I WAS THE LITTLE BOY IN ROW 2, SEAT 12 WHO'D JUST FALLEN IN LOVE WITH THE NEW YORK METS.

I'LL NEVER FORGET THAT FIRST GAME:

I CLOSED MY EYES AND WENT FOR EVERY POP FLY THAT CAME NEAR US...

...EVEN THE ONES THAT LANDED TWENTY ROWS BACK.

NOW REMEMBER: WE CAN'T SIP OUR SODA UNTIL THE CATCHER THROWS TO SECOND BASE OR WE LOSE THE GAME. YOU GOT YOUR RALLY CAP ON, KILLER?

YUP.

I ABSORBED IT ALL--THE RALLY CAPS, THE FOUL BALLS, THE STRATEGY... EVEN THOUGH I DIDN'T UNDERSTAND ANY OF IT.

I THOUGHT THE SEVENTH INNING STRETCH WAS WHERE EVERYONE TOOK A NAP FOR A HALF HOUR AND RESUMED PLAY LATER ON.

BY THE NINTH INNING, THE GAME WAS WELL IN HAND. MY HEROES WERE AHEAD BY THREE RUNS. THE PITCHING COACH WAS SENT OUT TO BRING IN OUR CLOSER, JUST SO THE GUY COULD GET SOME WORK IN.

AND MOMENTS LATER, IT HAPPENED: LONGEST HOME RUN IN THE HISTORY OF SHEA STADIUM.

GRAND SLAM. FOUR RUNS.

METS *LOSE.*

WHAT'S WRONG, KILLER? YOU DIDN'T LIKE THE GAME?

I'M NOT COMIN' HERE AGAIN. THIS *BLOWS.*

LOOK, PETEY...IT'S OKAY-- REALLY, IT IS. YOU CAN'T GET UPSET OVER ONE GAME. IF THE PLAYERS GOT UPSET AFTER EVERY LOSS, THEY'D HAVE TO RETIRE AND WORK ON HORSE FARMS OR SOMETHING.

YOU CAN'T ALWAYS WIN--THAT'S THE WAY LIFE WORKS. SOMETIMES, IT DOESN'T MATTER HOW HARD YOU TRY, YOU LOSE ANYWAY.

LISTEN, KILLER: LIFE IS A VERY LONG SEASON. SOME YOU WIN, SOME YOU LOSE...AND IT'S *GOOD* TO LOSE ONCE IN A WHILE. IT MAKES THE WINNING ALL THE SWEETER.

MAYBE NEXT YEAR, OKAY? WE'LL COME AGAIN AND SEE IF THEY WIN. THAT OKAY WITH YOU?

OKAY.

OVER TIME, THAT CAME TO BE KNOWN AS *"THE SPEECH,"* ON ACCOUNT OF HOW THE METS WOULD LOSE IN DIABOLICAL FASHION EVERY TIME WE ATTENDED OUR YEARLY GAME.

"MAYBE NEXT YEAR" BECAME OUR MANTRA.

SOMETIMES, IT'D BE A NINE-RUN BLOWOUT IN THE FIRST INNING. OTHER TIMES, THE CLOSER WOULD BE STRUCK WITH A CASE OF SPONTANEOUS CRAP-ITIS JUST AS THEIR PINCH HITTER STEPPED TO THE PLATE.

OUR ONGOING ATTENDANCE BECAME AFFECTIONATELY KNOWN BETWEEN THE TWO OF US AS THE *"ANNUAL KISS OF DEATH TOUR."*

BY ABOUT OUR SIXTH OR SEVENTH YEAR OF COMING, I WAS CERTAIN THINGS COULDN'T GET ANY WORSE. THAT WAS BEFORE THE *MASCOT* INCIDENT--

OH, JEEZ...

THIS PARTICULAR YEAR, THE METS HAD GIVEN UP TWELVE RUNS IN THE FIRST INNING, THERE'D BEEN AT LEAST THREE MALE STREAKERS, AND THE MANAGER HAD ALREADY BEEN EJECTED FOR CARRYING A CONCEALED WEAPON...

DON'T WORRY, SON-- I THINK WE GOT 'EM ON THE ROPES THIS TIME. WE'RE ONLY DOWN BY TWENTY-FOUR RUNS. THERE'S ALMOST TWO INNINGS LEFT--

O-OKAY, UNCLE BEN.

KRAK

THAT WAS WHEN I SAW IT HEADED FOR ME, LIKE A GIANT ASTEROID ON A COLLISION COURSE WITH SCHOOLBOY DESTINY.

THIS WAS THE MOMENT I'D BEEN WAITING FOR--THE VERY REASON I'D BROUGHT MY GLOVE ALONG WITH ME ALL THESE YEARS. FINALLY, MY VERY OWN SOUVENIR!

I CLOSED MY EYES AND WAITED FOR MY PRIZE TO HIT THE BACK OF MY GLOVE.

BONK

OH, DEAR.

MEDIC! HEY, WE NEED A MEDIC OVER HERE--THIS KID JUST GOT BEANED!

HEY, BOSS, YOU SEE THAT? SOME KID JUST GOT WHACKED ON THE HEAD.

UHM...LISTEN, PERCY...CAN YOU GO OVER AND CHECK IT OUT, MAYBE DO SOME DAMAGE CONTROL?

BOSS SAYS WE GOTTA MAKE SURE THE CUSTOMERS DON'T GET SCARED WHEN THIS HAPPENS.

NO PROBLEMO. I'M ON IT.

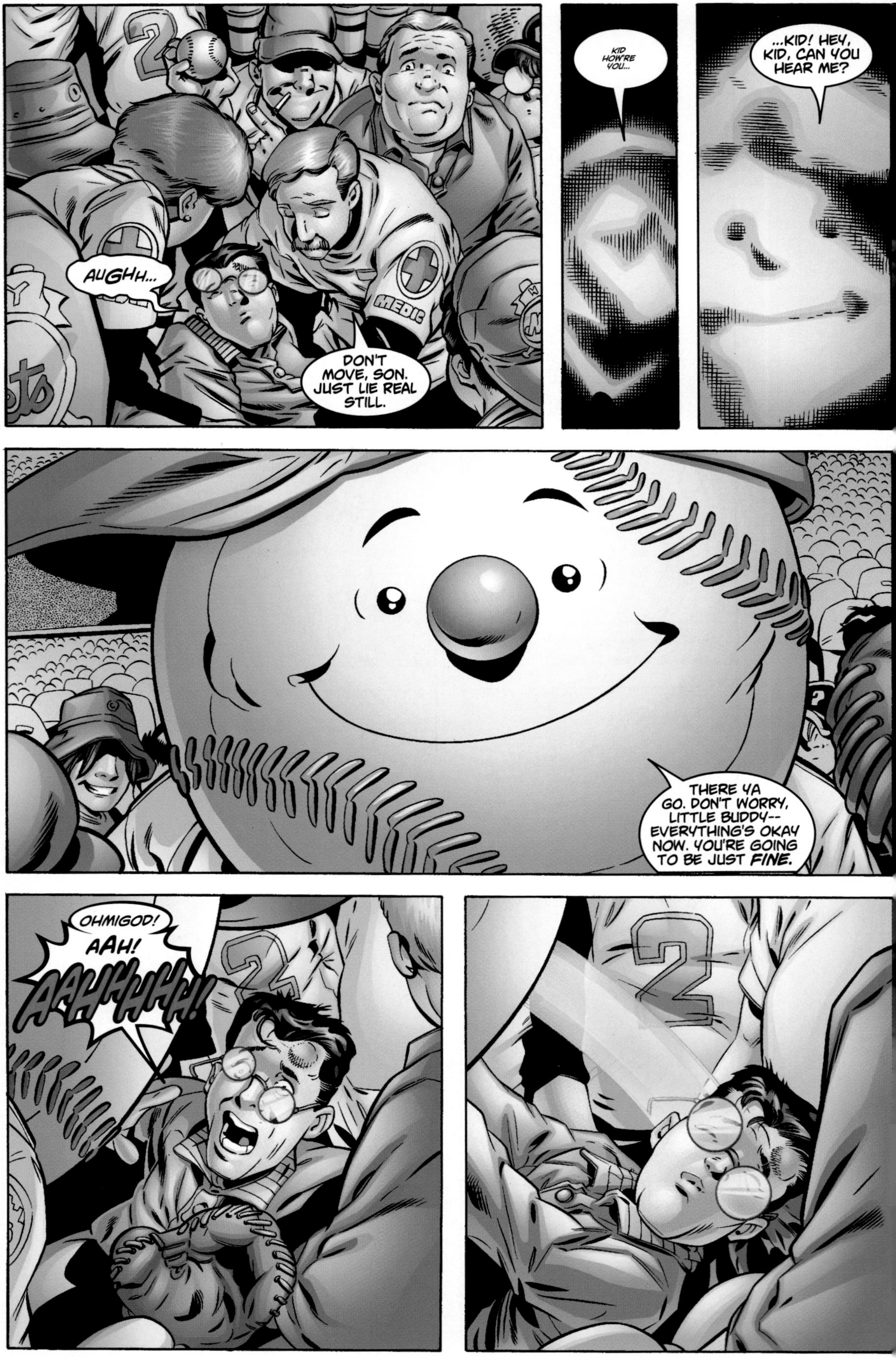
AUGHH...
DON'T MOVE, SON. JUST LIE REAL STILL.
KID HOW'RE YOU...
...KID! HEY, KID, CAN YOU HEAR ME?
THERE YA GO. DON'T WORRY, LITTLE BUDDY-- EVERYTHING'S OKAY NOW. YOU'RE GOING TO BE JUST *FINE.*
OHMIGOD!
AAH!
AAHHHHH!

WELL, AT LEAST I MADE THE PAPERS THE NEXT DAY--MY BEANING WAS THE HIGHLIGHT OF THE GAME, APPARENTLY.

IN OTHER NEWS, THE METS LOST BY THIRTY RUNS, OUR FIRST BASEMAN BLEW HIS ARM OUT PITCHING RELIEF, AND THE *OWNER* WAS EJECTED FOR CHARGING THE MOUND.

THANKFULLY, I REMEMBERED NONE OF IT. AND, AS AN ADDED BONUS, I DIDN'T HAVE TO LISTEN TO "THE SPEECH."

NOT THAT I DON'T REMEMBER IT EVEN TO THIS DAY, WORD FOR WORD. IT'S STAYED WITH ME ALL THIS TIME.

I STILL SWING BY HERE SOMETIMES WHEN THINGS ARE QUIET IN THE CITY. JUST TO CATCH A COUPLE OF INNINGS AND REFLECT ON WHY I DO WHAT I DO.

AND WHEN I LOOK DOWN AT THE CROWD, I'M ALWAYS REMINDED OF ONE VERY *IMPORTANT* DAY...

HEY PETEY...RISE AND SHINE, IT'S BASEBALL TIME.

I FEEL GOOD ABOUT TODAY-- I THINK THIS COULD *FINALLY* BE THE YEAR.

OH, YOU BOYS AND YOUR SPORTS!

WHAT'S THE PROBLEM, KILLER? NOT HUNGRY?

I DON'T KNOW IF I WANNA GO THIS YEAR, UNCLE BEN. IT'S KIND OF A *DRAG.*

OKAY, PAL-- I UNDERSTAND. I'LL JUST GO BY *MYSELF,* THEN...

UH...NO NEED, UNCLE BEN. I'LL BE READY IN A MINUTE, OKAY?

I ACTED LIKE A PILL THE ENTIRE WAY TO THE STADIUM, MAKING IT CLEAR THAT I'D RATHER BE ANYWHERE BUT THERE. I WAS GETTING OLDER, BUT SO WAS HE. YOU COULD TELL WE WERE DRIFTING *APART*...

HEY, BUDDY, SEE THE *BLIMP*? *THAT'S* A FIRST! AND I HEAR THEY PAINTED THE TOPS OF THE DUGOUTS!

I TOLD YOU TODAY WAS GOING TO BE DIFFERENT. DIDN'T I *SAY* SO?

THERE YA GO...OUR USUAL SEATS, M'LUD! I LIKE THE LOOK OF OUR LINEUP THIS YEAR. I THINK WE CAN DO SOME DAMAGE IN THE MIDDLE OF THE ORDER--

WHATEVER. THEY'LL STILL LOSE.

WELL, IT DOESN'T MATTER IF THEY DO--IT'S *GOOD* TO LOSE ONCE IN A WHILE. IT MAKES WINNING ALL THE--

UNCLE BEN, HOW ABOUT WE SKIP THE SPEECH THIS YEAR, OKAY?

AS YOU *LIKE*, PETER.

AND SO I SAT THERE FEELING BAD, AND HE SAT THERE TO THE LEFT OF ME IN SILENCE. AND TOGETHER THE TWO OF US WATCHED THE METS GET BLOWN OUT, TWO FEET AWAY AND FIVE MILES APART.

BUT YOU KNOW, A FUNNY THING HAPPENED ON THE WAY TO YET ANOTHER DEVILISH DEFEAT...

...THE METS ACTUALLY STARTED TO *WIN*.

I DON'T BELIEVE IT! I DON'T BELIEVE IT! WE *WON*!

UNCLE BEN, DID YOU SEE--?

BUT HE DIDN'T HAVE TO SAY A WORD. THE WHOLE MESSAGE OF THE MOMENT WAS WRITTEN ON HIS FACE.

YEAH...I GET IT. LIFE'S A VERY LONG SEASON. SOME YOU WIN...

AND JUST FOR TODAY, WE WERE WINNERS--ME AND MY UNCLE BEN, SHARING A MOMENT IN THE SEATS OF SHEA STADIUM.

THE METS HAD FINALLY *WON*. SUDDENLY, LIFE MADE COMPLETE SENSE TO ME.

THREE DAYS LATER, HE WAS *DEAD*.

GOD, I *MISS* THAT OLD MAN.

THAT'S WHY I COME HERE EVERY YEAR-- NOT TO WATCH THE GAME, BUT TO CONNECT TO THE GOOFY OLD GUY WHO BROUGHT ME HERE FOR THE FIRST TIME. IT'S HOW I CONNECT WITH *MYSELF.*

WHAT, YOU COULDN'T HAVE MANAGED A *RAINOUT* OR SOMETHING, YOU OLD CODGER?

I SUDDENLY REALIZE THAT I'M ALONE IN THE STANDS AND IT'S GETTING *COLD.* THE METS HAVE LOST BY TWELVE BILLION RUNS. NOT THAT THE SCORE MAKES ANY DIFFERENCE.

I MEAN, AT LEAST OUR CATCHER MADE THE ALL-STAR TEAM THIS YEAR. AND BESIDES IT'S A *LONG* SEASON.

AH, WELL...TIME TO PUT THE OLD GLOVE AWAY FOR ANOTHER YEAR, I GUESS. AS I TRUDGE TOWARDS THE EMPTY EXIT ROWS, SOMETHING MAKES ME STOP FOR A MOMENT AND LOOK BACK.

MAYBE IT'S JUST THE SOUND OF THE WIND BLOWING THE TRASH AROUND. MAYBE IT'S NOTHING... BUT I COULD SWEAR IT SOUNDS LIKE AN OLD MAN'S VOICE, WHISPERING ACROSS THE YEARS:

STAN LEE presents:

Maybe Next Year

PAUL JENKINS writer
MARK BUCKINGHAM pencils
WAYNE FAUCHER inks
TRANSPARENCY DIGITAL colorist
RS & COMICRAFT's Jason letterer
JOHN MIESEGAES assistant editor
AXEL ALONSO editor
JOE QUESADA editor in chief
BILL JEMAS president

AH-HUHH... ≥HUFF≥...

EXCUSE ME, PLEASE. *SORRY* --

...HHH... ≥AUHH≥...

BROTHER *RICHARD!* BROTHER *RICHARD!*

NO ONE HERE HAS TAKEN A VOW OF *SILENCE,* BROTHER IAN, BUT WE HAVEN'T TAKEN A VOW OF *SHOUTING* EITHER. I REALIZE YOU'RE NEW TO OUR MONASTERY BUT --

BROTHER RICHARD, *PLEASE...*

OH, *NO.*

WHEN DID IT *HAPPEN?*

I-I'M NOT SURE. A FEW MINUTES AGO, MAYBE MORE.

IAN, I DON'T NEED TO REMIND YOU JUST HOW *SERIOUS* THIS IS. HAVE YOU SEARCHED THE GROUNDS FULLY?

...≀HUFF≀... NOT *YET.* WE DIDN'T... EHH... WE DIDN'T HAVE TIME TO REACT...

...HHH... ONE MOMENT, EVERYTHING WAS PEACEFUL... ≀HUFF≀... THE NEXT, HE WAS *GONE* --

HELLO -- IS ANYBODY *THERE?* CAN YOU *HEAR* ME DOWN THERE?

OH, GOD HAVE MERCY ON US ALL.

Paul Jenkins writer Mark Buckingham pencils Wayne Faucher inks Transparency Digital colors
RS & Comicraft letters John Miesegaes ass't ed. Axel Alonso editor Joe Quesada chief Bill Jemas president

If Thine Eyes Offend Thee...

I THINK THEY'RE JUST *DARLING!*

SALT AND PEPPER SHAKERS FOR YOUR NEW HOME! I PICKED THEM UP FOR A *SONG* AT A RUMMAGE SALE AND NATURALLY THOUGHT OF YOU, PETER.

YEAH. *NATURALLY.*

WELL, WHAT DO YOU THINK? DO YOU *LIKE* THEM?

YEAH, THEY'RE UH...

REVOLTING.

...*NICE.* YOU DON'T THINK THIS BROKEN ONE'S A BIT *WOBBLY,* AUNT MAY? ONLY I WOULDN'T WANT IT TO GET *BROKEN,* OR ANYTHING --

YOU KNOW, IF YOU DON'T LIKE THEM, PETER, YOU COULD JUST *TELL* ME. I WOULDN'T BE OFFENDED --

OF *COURSE* HE LIKES THEM. THEY'RE PERFECT.

WELL, *HELLO,* DEAR... ARE YOU A FRIEND OF PETER'S? I'M HIS AUNT MAY.

OH, *YOU'RE* THE LOVELY AUNT MAY? I'VE HEARD SO MUCH ABOUT YOU!

YOU HAVE? WELL NOW... I WONDER WHY I'VE NEVER HEARD ABOUT *YOU?* PETER, HAVE YOU BEEN HIDING YOUR GIRLFRIENDS FROM YOUR STUFFY OLD AUNT AGAIN?

AW, YOU KNOW HOW *SHY* HE CAN BE SOMETIMES, AUNT MAY. I'M *CARYN,* BY THE WAY -- I LIVE ACROSS THE ALLEY.

LISTEN, PETER... I JUST POPPED BY TO THANK YOU FOR LOOKING AFTER BARKER WHILE I WAS GONE.

ANYWAY, I WAS THINKING SINCE THEY'VE GOT THAT BIG FUNFAIR SET UP IN CENTRAL PARK, MAYBE WE COULD GO CHECK IT OUT? *MY* TREAT.

RIGHT. UM. WELL, I'D *LOVE* TO, Y'KNOW, CARYN... UH...

...BUT I HAVE A BUNCH OF PAPERS TO MARK FOR SCHOOL.

THEY'RE DUE ON *FRIDAY.*

OH, PETER, SOMETIMES YOU CAN BE SUCH AN OLD *FUDDY-DUDDY!* THIS LOVELY YOUNG LADY OFFERS TO TAKE YOU TO THE FAIR... ANY BOY WITH HALF A MIND WOULD *JUMP* AT THE CHANCE!

RIGHT ON.

CLUNK

SURE.

QUICKLY! TO THE *MONKMOBILE*, BROTHER IAN! I'LL DRIVE. YOU KEEP A LOOKOUT FOR HIM OUT OF THE WINDOW --

ST FRAN

BUT WHERE WOULD HE *GO*, RICHARD? HE DOESN'T KNOW ANYTHING ABOUT THE CITY --

HE KNOWS ENOUGH FROM WHAT HE'S SEEN ON THE TELEVISION, BROTHER. WE'RE GOING TO HAVE TO TRACK HIM DOWN BEFORE HE DOES ANY SERIOUS DAMAGE.

SHOULD WE ALERT THE AUTHORITIES?

NO! THEY WOULDN'T UNDERSTAND. HE'S MORE OF A DANGER TO HIMSELF THAN TO OTHERS.

BUT WHAT IF HE MAKES *CONTACT* WITH ANYONE, BROTHER? WHAT THEN?

"THEN, WE PRAY."

I DUNNO -- HE AIN'T GOT NO *LETTERS* ON 'IM LIKE THAT OLD GUY DID. LET'S GIVE IT A SHOT --

GOING SOMEWHERE?

Y-YES... WILLIAM IS WALKING TO THE PARK.

KINDA *DARK* T' BE WEARIN' THEM HEAVY SHADES, HUH, *"WILLIAM"*? WHAT SAY I *CARRY* 'EM FOR YOU? I'LL CARRY ALL YOUR *CASH* AS WELL, IF YOU LIKE --

AAH!

C'MON, TERRY. THERE'S PEOPLE *COMIN'* --

UHH... PLEASE... WILLIAM IS *AFRAID.* THIS IS VERY *BAD.*

BAD FOR *YOU,* BLIND BOY --

JEEZ! LOOK AT HIS *EYES!*

BOOM

WILLIAM IS *SORRY.*

AH, YES... WHAT COULD BE *LESS* EXCRUCIATING THAN WALKING THROUGH A FUNFAIR WITH A BEAUTIFUL GIRL ON MY ARM AND A NEAR-EMPTY WALLET IN MY POCKET?

THE ANSWER, OF COURSE, IS "A RED-HOT POKER IN THE EYE." I MEAN, CARYN'S A SWEET ENOUGH PERSON BUT I CAN'T TELL IF SHE'S OBLIVIOUS OR DEVIOUS OR *BOTH*.

Little Devil HOOPLA

TEST YOUR STRENGTH

PROBABLY OPTION "C"; A TOTAL *WHACKO*. IT'S FUNNY, THOUGH, HOW IN THAT RESPECT SHE REMINDS ME OF...

...MARY JANE.

I'M WONDERING HOW I'M GOING TO POLITELY SPURN THE POOR KID. AND IT'S JUST AS I'M ABOUT TO GIVE UP THAT I'M GIVEN FINAL *PROOF* THE UNIVERSE EXISTS ONLY TO TORMENT ME...

I DUNNO... I COULDA *SWORN* I SAW PETER JUST A MOMENT AGO...

WHAT'S UP, HONEY-BEE?

OH, SH -- -- ERR... NOTHING.

SAY, CARYN... LET'S TRY IN *HERE* --

ARCHERY

TEST YOUR SKILL! WIN A BIG BEAR!

OOH, *COOL!* WIN ME A PRIZE, YOU BIG STUD, YOU!

HERE. THREE ARROWS FER FIVE BUCKS. YOU C'N HAVE SEVEN FER *TEN*, IF Y'LIKE --

UH, YEAH...RIGHT. WHATEVER.

ANYWHERE IN THE BULL WINS A SMALL PRIZE. DEAD IN THE CENTER FER TH' BIG ONE. *DEAD* CENTER, MIND!

TOP PRIZE

DON'T WORRY, I'M GOOD AT THIS. SEE, IT'S ALL IN THE RELEASE -- ALL YOU DO IS PULL BACK, LIKE THIS...

...AN' THEN, YOU LET YOUR BREATH GO. AN' THEN...

...GOTTA BE AROUND HERE SOME-WHERE...

...AN' THEN...

THWANGG

OY!

WHAT, YOU THINK THA'S *FUNNY?*

NICE *SHOT*, ROBIN HOOD.

TOP PRIZE

YOU GOTTA *PAY* FER THAT!

WELL, YOU DID SAY "DEAD CENTER" --

AAAAAAH! EEEEEEK!

HEY, WHAT'S GOING ON OUT THERE --?

OMIGOD! HE'S *CRAZY!*

DID YOU SEE HIS EYES?

...I DUNNO, SOME KINDA LASER SHOW WENT WRONG, OR SOMETHIN'...

PETER! PETER -- AWWK!

GET BACK! HE'S COMIN' THIS WAY!

WELL, *THAT'S* A FIRST: SAVED BY A RAMPAGING *CROWD.*

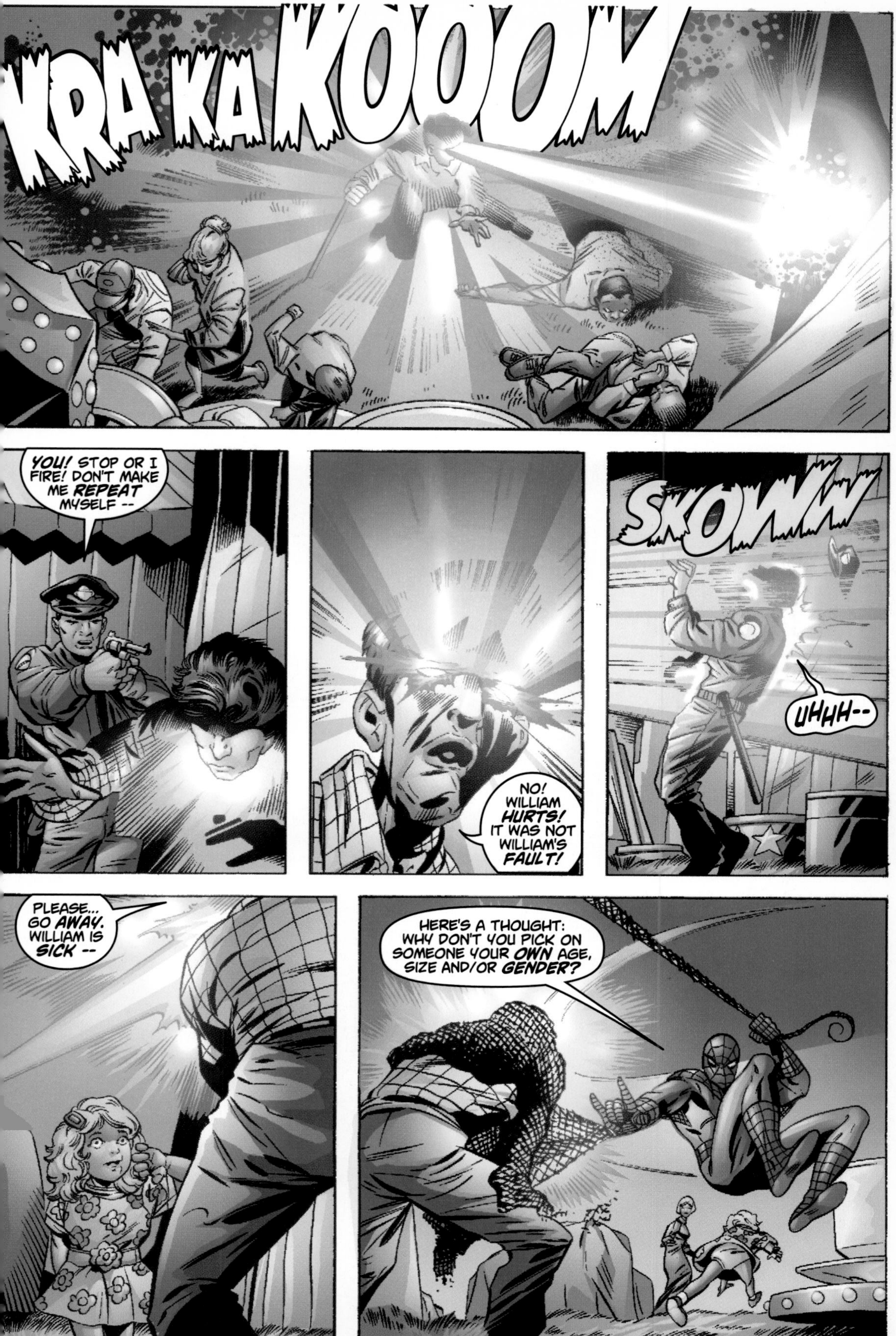
KRA KA KOOOM
YOU! STOP OR I FIRE! DON'T MAKE ME REPEAT MYSELF --
NO! WILLIAM HURTS! IT WAS NOT WILLIAM'S FAULT!
SKOWW
UHHH--
PLEASE... GO AWAY. WILLIAM IS SICK --
HERE'S A THOUGHT: WHY DON'T YOU PICK ON SOMEONE YOUR OWN AGE, SIZE AND/OR GENDER?

THOOOM

CONJUNCTIVITIS, HUH? THAT *BLOWS*, DUDE.

WHAT SAY YOU AN' ME GO FIND A DOCTOR AND CLEAR IT UP? THAT WAY, NO ONE ELSE GETS HURT.

...NNN... WILLIAM DOES NOT WANT TO... WILLIAM IS GOING FOR A WALK. TO A *SPECIAL PLACE.*

WITH A FISH

THAT WOULD BE "PRISON," WILLIAM. AND SPIDER-MAN IS GOING TO MAKE SURE WILLIAM GETS THERE SAFE AND *SOUND* --

NN-AAH! IT HURTS! NO TIME!

ZZZTT

WHAM

YOW!

I MAY BE *QUICK* -- I MEAN, YOU'RE LOOKING AT THE DUDE WHO LEFT BILLY PINDER IN THE DUST DURING A SECOND GRADE SACK RACE!

ADMITTEDLY, HE WAS FIFTY YARDS BACK AND HURLING UP AN EGG SANDWICH AT THE TIME, BUT I DIGRESS. ANYWAY... I MAY BE *QUICK* --

-- BUT I THINK IT WAS EINSTEIN, OR SOMEONE, WHO SAID, "*YOU CAN'T RUN FASTER THAN THE SPEED OF LIGHT.*"

ZZ-TTT

UHH...

THUMP

OW... THIS GUY'S *DYNAMITE* --

A-ARE YOU SPIDER-MAN?

UM. WE'RE NOT LOOKING FOR TROUBLE. WE JUST NEED TO *TALK* TO YOU, THAT'S ALL.

IT'S ABOUT *WILLIAM.*

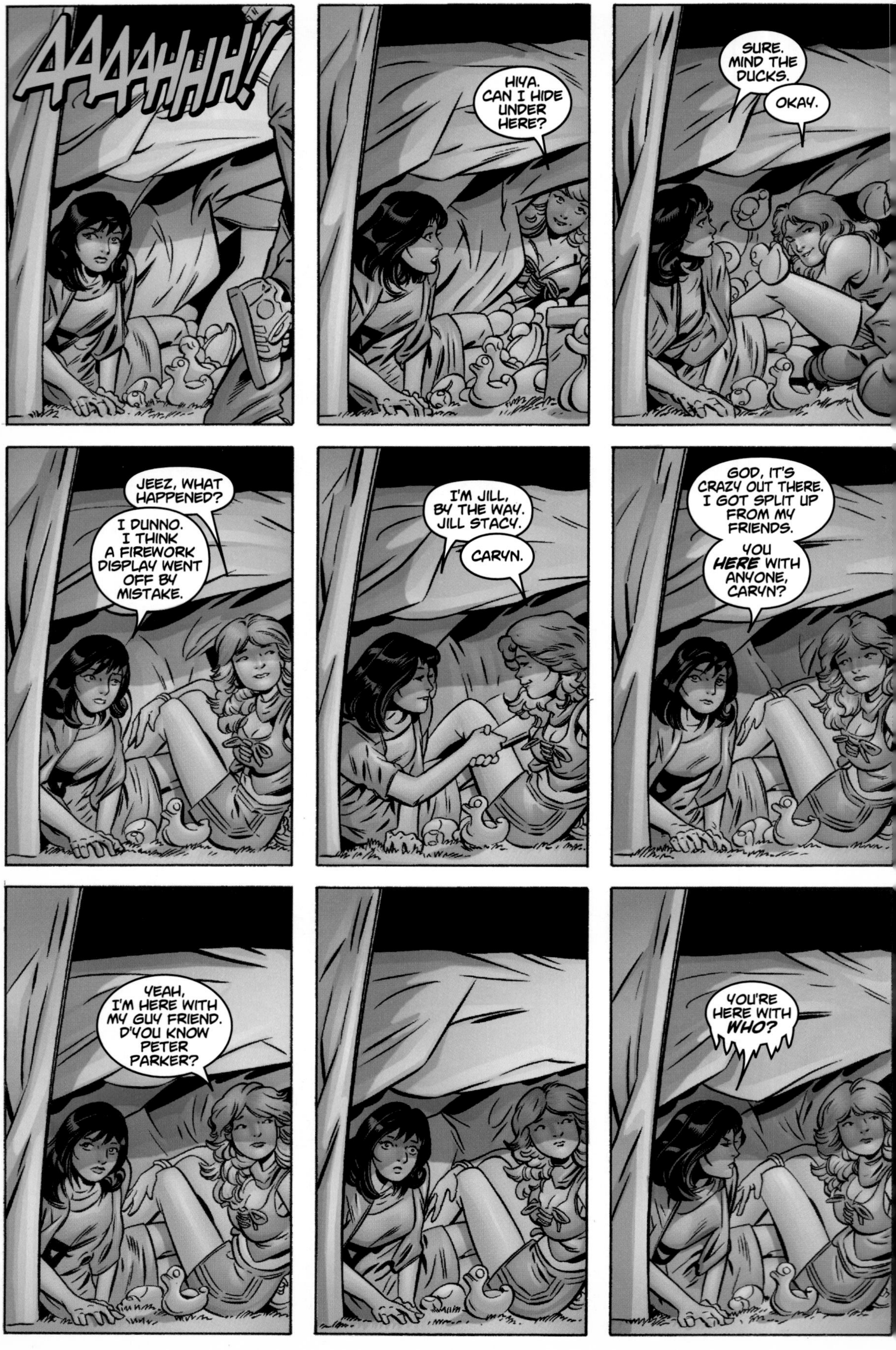
AAAAHHH!!
HIYA. CAN I HIDE UNDER HERE?
SURE. MIND THE DUCKS.
OKAY.
JEEZ, WHAT HAPPENED?
I DUNNO. I THINK A FIREWORK DISPLAY WENT OFF BY MISTAKE.
I'M JILL, BY THE WAY. JILL STACY.
CARYN.
GOD, IT'S CRAZY OUT THERE. I GOT SPLIT UP FROM MY FRIENDS.
YOU **HERE** WITH ANYONE, CARYN?
YEAH, I'M HERE WITH MY GUY FRIEND. D'YOU KNOW PETER PARKER?
YOU'RE HERE WITH **WHO?**

OKAY, SO... BY "WILLIAM" YOU WOULD MEAN THE SUPERLOON WITH THE EYEBALLS WHO KEEPS CALLING HIMSELF *WILLIAM*, RIGHT?

YES, THAT'S HIM. WILLIAM'S NOT GOING TO HURT ANYONE, SPIDER-MAN -- AT LEAST, NOT *INTENTIONALLY*.

I KNOW IT LOOKS BAD... BUT THE EFFECTS OF HIS EYE-BEAMS ARE ONLY *TEMPORARY*. IT'S MORE DANGEROUS TO WILLIAM THAN TO HIS VICTIMS. PLEASE, LET ME *EXPLAIN*...

"WILLIAM WAS BROUGHT TO US WHEN HE WAS A BABY -- LEFT WITH NO NOTE OF EXPLANATION AT THE DOOR OF OUR ORPHANAGE. HIS EYES WERE BANDAGED, SO WE NATURALLY ASSUMED HE'D BEEN INJURED.

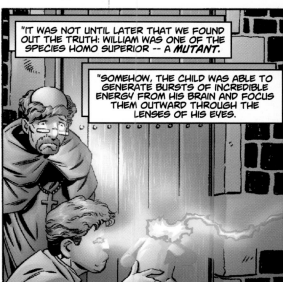

"IT WAS NOT UNTIL LATER THAT WE FOUND OUT THE TRUTH: WILLIAM WAS ONE OF THE SPECIES HOMO SUPERIOR -- A *MUTANT.*

"SOMEHOW, THE CHILD WAS ABLE TO GENERATE BURSTS OF INCREDIBLE ENERGY FROM HIS BRAIN AND FOCUS THEM OUTWARD THROUGH THE LENSES OF HIS EYES.

"BUT THERE WAS A PROBLEM: THE OUTBURSTS WERE DETRIMENTAL TO WILLIAM'S HEALTH. IF THE BOY LAY ON HIS BACK, HE WAS ABLE TO OPEN HIS EYES WITH NO ILL EFFECTS...

"BUT WHEN STANDING OR UPRIGHT, WILLIAM'S EYES HAD TO REMAIN CLOSED AT ALL TIMES.

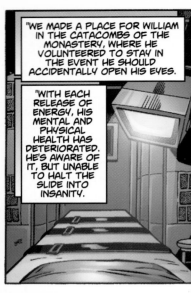

"WE MADE A PLACE FOR WILLIAM IN THE CATACOMBS OF THE MONASTERY, WHERE HE VOLUNTEERED TO STAY IN THE EVENT HE SHOULD ACCIDENTALLY OPEN HIS EYES.

"WITH EACH RELEASE OF ENERGY, HIS MENTAL AND PHYSICAL HEALTH HAS DETERIORATED. HE'S AWARE OF IT, BUT UNABLE TO HALT THE SLIDE INTO INSANITY.

"AND SO, WE PROVIDE FOR HIM AS BEST WE CAN. WE WATCH, HELPLESS, AS THE POOR CHILD ENDURES ENDLESS DAYS ON HIS BACK WITH ONLY A TELEVISION AS HIS EYES TO THE OUTSIDE WORLD.

"IMAGINE BEING PERFECTLY ABLE TO *UNDERSTAND* GOD'S SUBLIME CREATION BUT UNABLE TO *EXPERIENCE* IT. TO SPEND ONE'S LIFE IN SADNESS, STRAPPED TO A TABLE FOR THE PROTECTION ON OTHERS.

"THAT WAS WILLIAM'S CHOICE."

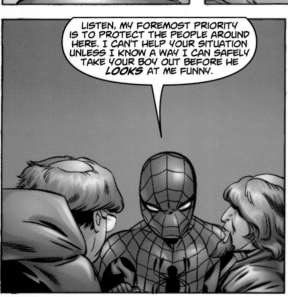

LISTEN, MY FOREMOST PRIORITY IS TO PROTECT THE PEOPLE AROUND HERE. I CAN'T HELP YOUR SITUATION UNLESS I KNOW A WAY I CAN SAFELY TAKE YOUR BOY OUT BEFORE HE *LOOKS* AT ME FUNNY.

PLEASE, SPIDER-MAN -- A MAN OF YOUR ABILITIES SHOULD BE ABLE TO UNDERSTAND. WILLIAM DIDN'T WANT THIS POWER OF HIS -- TO HIM, IT'S A *CURSE.*

IF HE STANDS WITH HIS EYES OPEN FOR A LONG PERIOD OF TIME, THE EXPELLED ENERGY SEEMS TO *DRAIN* HIM.

WE DON'T KNOW WHY HE SUDDENLY DECIDED TO COME HERE. CLEARLY, HE HAS SOMETHING IN MIND, BUT HE DIDN'T COMMUNICATE IT TO US.

HIS MIND'S BECOMING UNHINGED -- YOU MUST GET TO HIM BEFORE HE HURTS HIMSELF.

WHAT D'YOU NEED ME TO DO?

CLOSE HIS EYES -- *SOMEHOW.* IF HE STANDS WITH THEM OPEN FOR TOO MUCH LONGER, HE'S GOING TO *DIE.*

AS I SWING OVER THE TWISTED METAL AND BURNING CANVAS THAT USED TO BE A FUNFAIR, I REALIZE THE ENERGY BLASTS ARE INTENSIFYING.

ALL THAT RELEASE IS HAVING A NEGATIVE EFFECT ON WILLIAM'S MIND. HE'S COMING *APART*.

BOOM

AND I CAN'T HELP WONDERING WHAT IT WOULD BE LIKE TO GO THROUGH THAT ORDEAL. THERE'S A SCHOOL OF THOUGHT THAT SAYS WITH GREAT POWER COMES GREAT RESPONSIBILITY.

BUT WHAT IF YOU NEVER *WANTED* POWER?

HEY, WILLIAM! OVER HERE, BUD! LOOK OVER HERE!

NO.

ZZZZZZZZZZZZZ

CONTROL PANEL

C'MON, WILLIAM. YOU GOTTA STOP NOW, I CAN *HELP* YOU --

URHH--

WILLIAM DOESN'T WANT HELP. THIS IS THE PLACE WILLIAM SAW ON TV.

WILLIAM WANTS TO *SEE*.

WAIT!

SUDDENLY, I UNDERSTAND WHAT'S HE'S TRYING TO DO. THE WALL OF DEATH BEGINS TO SPIN AT AN IMPOSSIBLE RATE AND AS IT DOES SO, THE GRAVITATIONAL FORCES SLAM WILLIAM TO ITS SIDE.

NOW, THE MACHINE ELEVATES... WITH IT'S LONE OCCUPANT LYING DOWN... AND *STANDING* AT THE SAME TIME!

WHAT HAPPENED? WHERE IS HE?

IN THERE! HE FUSED THE CONTROL BOX!

AAH! AAH! AAH! AAH! AAH! AAH!

HE'S GONNA LIQUEFY IN THERE. I NEED YOU TWO TO TRY AND STOP THE ROTATION, MAYBE CUT OFF THE POWER SUPPLY.

I'M GOING IN!

THUD

UHH--!

OKAY, SPIDEY... NOW WHAT?

YYEESSSSS...

...HHH... HOLD ON...

YES... THERE...!

HELLO, STARS. WILLIAM SEES YOU.

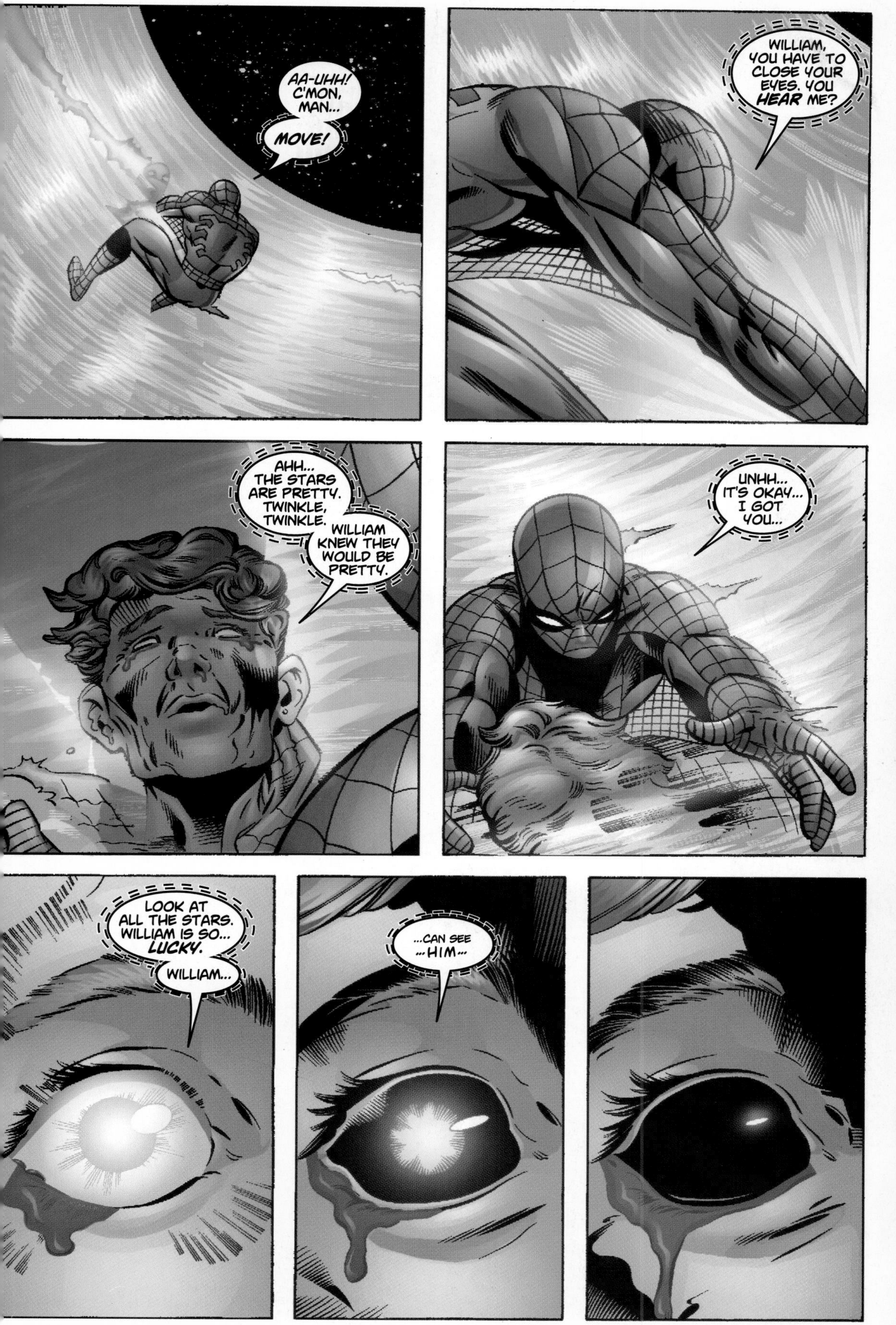
AA-UHH! C'MON, MAN...
MOVE!
WILLIAM, YOU HAVE TO CLOSE YOUR EYES. YOU HEAR ME?
AHH... THE STARS ARE PRETTY. TWINKLE, TWINKLE.
WILLIAM KNEW THEY WOULD BE PRETTY.
UNHH... IT'S OKAY... I GOT YOU...
LOOK AT ALL THE STARS. WILLIAM IS SO... LUCKY.
WILLIAM...
...CAN SEE ...HIM...

HE'S GONE.

SPINNING INTO THE VOID LIKE WATER DOWN A DRAIN.

WITHOUT THE STRENGTH TO MOVE AWAY, I STRAIN MY NECK AGAINST THE IMPOSSIBLE PULL OF THE SPINNING MACHINE, AND I TRY TO SEE WHAT WILLIAM SAW.

BUT ALL I SEE ARE LITTLE POINTS OF LIGHT AGAINST A BIG, BLACK BLANKET. A VAST SHROUD OF *NOTHING*, INFINITELY FAR AWAY.

SOMETIMES, I WISH I COULD BE AS LUCKY AS *WILLIAM*.